Contents

Firstly . . .		7
Introduction		9
1.	Life Sucks	11
2.	Designs on You	21
3.	Secret Spiders	34
4.	Who's Who?	44
5.	Headline News	55
6.	Boo!	63
7.	What a Blunderful World	71
8.	Crime of Passion	81
9.	Way to Go	94
10.	What a Pain	105
11.	Just Desserts	116
12.	Believe it or Not	126
13.	Grateful Dead	141
14.	Mathematical Certainty	152
15.	The Game of Life	165
16.	It's a Plot	177
	Notes	188

beyond belief?

PETER MEADOWS AND JOSEPH STEINBERG
with DONNA VANN

WORD PUBLISHING

WORD ENTERTAINMENT LTD

BEYOND BELIEF?

Copyright © 1999 Peter Meadows, Joseph Steinberg and Donna Vann

First published 1999 by Word Publishing
a division of Word Entertainment Ltd, 9 Holdom Avenue, Bletchley, Milton Keynes, Bucks, MK1 1QR, UK.

Reprinted 1999, 2000 (twice), 2001

ISBN 1 86024 321 5

Produced for Word Publishing by
Bookprint Creative Services. P.O. Box 827, BN21 3YJ, England.
Printed in Great Britain

beyond belief?

Firstly . . .

Authors usually like to put a few words at the front of their book to share the credit and ease their guilt. And here they are.

First, the credit. Though the voice you hear as you read is mine, this has been a remarkable team effort. Three of us – Joseph Steinberg, Donna Vann and myself – have shared the writing. Bouncing hither and thither – mostly by courtesy of the Internet – have been concepts, outlines, drafts and final text. It's been like playing tri-cornered ping-pong.

Of course, the buck has to stop somewhere – and it has been with me. But ask 'who wrote what' and you'll receive the answer 'all of us did'. So the 'author' has eleven children, has lived and worked in more than a dozen countries and all but one continent, and spent over 80 years following the road this book points to.

Credit also goes to a wider team. People like Roger Vann, who was intimately involved with the process from the start. And the myriad of others – ancient and modern – whose thoughts and words we have plundered to create the riches of what follows.

Second, the guilt. Overwhelming thanks go to those close to us who have paid the price of our absorption and endless working into the night during this elephantine pregnancy – particularly two wives, Rosemary and Jane. And the wider families of all of us.

A big thank you also to Jan Todd who managed the manuscript so efficiently under such pressure. And to our publishers, where the faith and patience of Nigel and Malcolm have been outstanding.

Our goal was to craft a down-to-earth book for 'ordinary', sane and sensible people about the issues of life. Why are we here? What really matters? Where are we going? And we have had such fun doing so.

Each of us have our favourite bits of the book. The wayward supermarket trolley, the day it was midnight, the plastic man and the windmill thing, the death of Friedrich, the tin squash ball, the bra straps and buckets.

You will get to meet them soon. Here's hoping you enjoy them as much as we have.

Peter Meadows
February 1999

INTRODUCTION

The journey starts here

Is it 'beyond belief' to think there might be more to life than this?

Is it pure madness to claim that beyond all the pleasures our senses can give, there's still an adventure waiting? Is it laughable to say life might offer something beyond our four score years and a retirement home?

Is it naive to believe a dimension exists outside of this tangible, touchable world? Or that human life is like a goldfish bowl, beyond which there is a world awaiting our discovery?

Are such thoughts of 'more than this' just a vain display of human vanity or a desperate quest for significance? Are we simply too scared to face up to being nothing but a smudge on the windscreen of time?

I don't know what's 'beyond belief' for you. Maybe it's the thought that God exists. Maybe it's the idea that life has an ultimate purpose. Maybe it's the notion that a very big Somebody out there cares whether you live or die or what happens to you in between.

Such issues are the territory of this book. The following pages offer you a journey of exploration into these great questions. If the truth is out there – about life, the universe and some other bits and bobs – it's worth finding. So let's see if we can nail it down.

I have no way of knowing how far down this road you've already travelled. Perhaps you see yourself as simply ticking the 'don't know' box – but with an open mind, ready to know if knowing is possible. Or you may have come some way down the track to shaping what is or isn't beyond belief for you.

Either way, please don't expect an unbiased excursion. As your guide, I own up readily to some firmly held conclusions – based on a journey of enquiry made over the past thirty years.

Indeed, the terrain you are about to scramble over has become familiar to me. And I have found it to have some wonderful 'views'. Views that, for me, became personal convictions which gradually and positively reshaped every aspect of my life – in a way I would have once considered beyond belief.

This has not been a lonely journey. Far from it. At this very moment my travelling companions number more than one and a half billion. They are spread right across the globe and are of every colour, social class and intellect.

Am I – and they – simply deluded? Or is there genuinely more to life?

Please suspend your honest disbelief for a while and let's go find out. Step this way. And watch out for the elephant dung.

Chapter 1

LIFE SUCKS

Is this all there is?

Sometimes, let's be honest, life sucks. It can be as much fun as stuffing marshmallows up your nose.

I'm reminded of a hamster and its owner. Each morning Sam hits the wheel, stopping only to snatch a bite to eat, driven on by some ingrained belief that all the effort is getting him somewhere. Trudge, trudge, trudge. Nibble, nibble, nibble. With only occasional treats to break the monotony. And for thirty-year-old Sam's pet hamster it is almost as bad!

Of course, life does have its great moments. We each spend enough money and energy making sure of that. The quest is for bigger, faster, glossier and newer. Toys for the girls as well as the boys. If only ageing could be delayed – and we could count on one day being an octogenarian sex machine – then life would be perfect. If only the anti-ageing cream could prolong teenage looks forever – and didn't taste so bad.

Yet, when we have conquered all known lands, accumulated all the possessions there are to be had, strolled the finest beaches in the world and finally figured out how to programme the video recorder – what then? When push comes to shove – and the last party popper has popped – where is the fizz? Suppose when we finally reach the top of the ladder we find it's leaning against the wrong wall?

Of course, some have life worse than others. Be grateful you were not born Martyn Eskins. This genius chose not to use a broom to remove cobwebs from his basement. Instead he used a propane torch – starting a fire that raged through his Ohio home.

Or show your admiration for the bravery of Canadians Daniel Kolta and Randy Taylor. They both met their end in a head-on collision – with each other. According to police in Windsor, Ontario, the two were playing a game of chicken with their snowmobiles.

Then there was Paul Stiller and his wife Bonnie – who landed in a New Jersey hospital. While driving around at 2 a.m., the bored couple lit a stick of dynamite and tried to toss it out the car window to see what would happen. But neither thought to wind down the window.

All these were recipients of runner-up prizes in the *Darwin Awards*. This annual honour goes to those who provide the universal human gene pool with the biggest service – by getting killed in the most extraordinarily stupid way.

And the winner? Roll the drums in memory of the 1998 recipient – Friedrich Riesfeldt. This unfortunate zoo-keeper from Paderborn in Germany, set out to solve the problem of a seriously constipated elephant. His solution involved a potent cocktail of twenty-two doses of animal laxative and more than a bushel of berries, figs and prunes. Not satisfied, the overzealous Fred then attempted to give the ailing elephant an olive-oil enema – at exactly the moment nature dramatically, and fatally, took its course.

The initial blast of Pachyderm poop knocked the unwary zoo-keeper to the ground, where he struck his head on a rock. There he lay unconscious – as the animal continued to evacuate another 200 pounds of animal excrement from its bowels. It was at least an hour before a watchman came along. By which time poor Fred – though warm and comfortable – had suffocated.

While life may never get that bad for us, we know what it is to live in a world of uncertainty and confusion. To plod through an existence of considerable pain but with little gain in real terms. Where 'OK' is often as good as it gets. Where the thought of life having an overall purpose and lasting fulfilment seldom has time even to enter our over-busy minds.

But sooner or later, probably when some event of life stops us in our tracks, the haunting thought nags away – 'Is this all there is?'

Our lives on a personal level

In the workplace we have longer hours, with fewer resources, greater insecurity and little likelihood of more money. Sound familiar?

Check these alarming statistics:

- Seven out of ten British workers want to put in only 40 hours a week. But the average employee works almost 45 hours a week – longer than any other nation in the European Union.
- One in four male employees works more than 48 hours a week. One in five manual workers puts in more than 50 hours. And one in eight managers works more than 60 hours.
- The average British lunch 'hour' is now only 30 minutes.
- One in ten of those who work get no paid holiday.

Ever wonder what those laboratory rats feel like while they try to work their way from one end of the maze to the other just to earn that little piece of cheese? Is it really that much different for us?

Meanwhile, our information 'rich' society bombards us with an ever-increasing deluge of spam. Messages we don't want or need are mingled with the constant barrage of phone calls, e-mail, faxes, Internet bulletins and even the occasional letter. In the end what does it all mean?

And whether you are a no-income, one- or two-income household, the pressure is relentlessly on to keep ahead. Who knows what the ill winds of the financial markets will blow our way? Where do you turn to find real security?

On the domestic front it's no less stressful. With so much going on you fear the moment when you take a child to the vet, the dog to the dentist, make coffee with gravy granules, fix your hair with furniture polish. And the dinner ends up on the ceiling.

Is it surprising that each working day, more than a quarter of a million people take time off because of stress-related illness? Or that insomnia has become a national epidemic?

Right now you are somewhere on the board game of life. Each day you roll the dice and move on. From driving licence to job, to flat, to a partner, to kids, to their education, to retirement, to decay, to . . . ? And when we finally 'win', then what? None of the trinkets we have accumulated can go with us. So what's it all about?

Our relationships

The trend is to marry later, co-habit more often and delay the arrival of children until the body clock has all but struck the midnight hour. And the medics are even working hard on that. How long before retirement homes need a nursery?!

Partners take each other for granted. As co-habitants, they maintain a pool-table existence – clicking into each other on occasions but mostly living in their own emotional 'pocket'.

'Till death us do part' becomes 'Until I get bored'. Partners skip out on each other and on their children, who increasingly carry the pain into their adult life. If it hasn't happened to us yet we wonder when it will. Or which rules our partner is playing to.

As a result, we now have a society where relationships have become almost as disposable as a razor blade. Once used, we're just tossed in the bin. That hurts.

Abuse within families – verbal, emotional, physical – has sadly become so common it scarcely shocks us any more.

The scars of broken relationships – even when there is no obvious betrayal – are not always on the outside. Break apart two bricks that have been cemented together and notice how each leaves parts of itself behind with the other. That's exactly how many of us can feel. Less complete. Less fulfilled. Undervalued, used, abused, and cast aside.

There's got to be more to life on a relational level than this.

Our lives in society

One of the key words sociologists are using when describing our society is 'anxiety'. It's easy to see why. So much of life is spiralling out of control.

For a start, we feel increasingly less safe – with CCTV cameras, mandatory mobile phones for after-dark vulnerable travellers and multiple locks on our doors all making the point.

My colleague Joseph Steinberg recently took a short holiday. Within eight days he discovered his Essex home had been burgled at least three times. In fact, the thieves kept coming back for more. The police found stuff stored by the back door ready for the next visit.

Joseph describes what he found as 'like the Goldilocks story gone horribly wrong'. The beds were messed up. The couch was slashed. The study was trashed. Drawer contents were poured out. Hamburgers lay uncooked on the grill. Beer cans and cigarette butts were strewn around. In a final ironic twist, one of the windows of his newly installed 'protect-your-home-better' double glazing had been removed to let the intruders in.

I went looking for a 'Sorry to Hear You Have Been Burgled' greeting card to cheer him up. They are not out yet. But they will be. Along with 'Smile, It's Only a Mugging!' and 'Best Wishes for the Safe Recovery of Your Car'.

We can't keep our property from being violated any more than we can keep others from violating the truth. Do you love each other? That was the question put to a newly engaged Charles and Diana. And his answer said it all. 'Of course. What ever love means.' To quote the Manic Street Preachers album title, 'This is My Truth – Tell Me Yours.'

So the Clintonesque question 'Are you having a sexual relationship?' comes down to 'It all depends what you mean by "are"'. Closer to home, downright lies become no more than being 'economical with the truth'.

That's all no big deal for us, maybe. But what about when the same values are applied to the food chain – as they have been. Ever eaten a hamburger? Then you're a candidate for Mad Cow Disease.

Quizzed over their statements to the public that eating beef was 'safe' the British Government had the perfect out. It was all a matter of 'what is meant by "safe"'. A more honest answer would have been, 'Safe compared to throwing yourself off the top of Big Ben with Maggie Thatcher strapped to your back.'

We no longer know what's true or what's safe. Is this all we have to look forward to?

Our lives on a global level

As if cows, cars and crime weren't bad enough, what about our planet? The picture is equally distressing.

Environmentally, human selfishness, greed and sheer stupidity is slowly turning a magnificent specimen into a wheezy out-of-condition mess. That's not me I'm talking about but our blue planet.

A random survey highlights the following facts:

- The hole in the ozone layer is so big you could drive a golf ball the size of the moon through it.
- Chunks of the South Pole the size of a small nation are breaking off.
- Radioactive waste dumped by the Soviet Union in Arctic seas is leaking through its containers, causing radiation levels to reach up to 100 times normal in some areas.
- Tons of waste dumped by a Taiwanese firm in Cambodia have created a mercury level thousands of times higher than safety standards permit – causing villagers nearby to complain of exhaustion and diarrhoea.

And when the scientific community starts to create 'bio-domes' to sustain life on Earth rather than Mars you know something has to be seriously wrong.

Economically, the world markets are braced for meltdown. To go overdrawn personally – or fail to make your credit card payments on time – is one thing. When an entire nation does it that's another. And they are, including great historic economies like Russia. When a small UK business goes bankrupt it is regrettable. But when all of Asia does the same that's another thing altogether!

At home, there are signs that pension payments will never be enough to meet our needs – even if the money we receive does not lose most of its value in some catastrophic global crash.

Internationally, war, conflict and terrorism become an increasing threat. More people have died in war or because of war over the past hundred years than in all the previous centuries combined.

Meanwhile, a cult unleashes deadly nerve gas in a capital city's underground system. And don't dare to leave your packed lunch unattended in a public place! It will spark off a major security alert and end in your cheese and pickle being blasted into a million fragments.

Historically, the dawn of a new millennium helps us assess our progress and our hope for the future. One newspaper commentator regards the twentieth century as 'the most murderous in recorded history and the most troubled politically and ethically'.[1] His conclusion is that, 'History will look at us, the creatures of the twentieth century, with horror.' He has good reason.

The past hundred years have seen:

- the greatest crime in recorded history – the murder of six million Jews
- two world wars; the first, when man learned to kill with the capacity of a slaughterhouse; the second, when civilians – women and children – as well as troops became legitimate targets

- a relentless stream of tyrants like Hitler, Stalin, Mao Tse-tung, Pol Pot, Amin, Pinochet and the rest
- incredible scientific advances such as cloning – but no moral framework with which to safeguard people from their abuse
- technological advances make the most degrading pornography available to anyone old enough to click a mouse.

History shows that the world entered the twentieth century with euphoria and great optimism. How different this time.

Are you feeling powerless yet? 'No,' you reply, 'I was feeling powerless before you started.' Feeling like a snowman in a deep fat fryer? Join the club.

Never have so many people felt such fear of the future or lack of satisfaction with the present.

A bigger picture?

Life seems beyond belief sometimes, doesn't it? Totally outside our control or ability to understand. So we keep our heads down and keep moving. Like Sam and his hamster.

But supposing – just supposing – there was a bigger picture. One that made sense of all we think we know already. One that could help us fulfil our deepest longings.

Perhaps you've seen that classic painting of the chubby angelic cherub, with plump face resting on even plumper hands and eyes reaching heavenwards in adoration. The face has become an icon – on greetings cards, place mats, framed pictures. And I'm entranced by it.

What a shock when I came across a print with not only this familiar heavenly being but a 'twin' alongside it. What a revelation to discover this cherub was part of a bigger picture. One I had never realised existed. And there was more.

This famous cherub – deservedly admired in its own right far and wide – makes up only a fraction of a magnificent painting by Raphael. Of course, I had been fully satisfied with the pleasure the little cherub gave me. But now I saw it was only a small detail of a larger work. Here was a whole world to be explored and enjoyed that was beyond my wildest dreams.

Could this be an expression of how life is? Could there be more outside the frame, a bigger picture you've never seen? Is it possible the 'God' you call on when things go wrong might really exist? And could this even be the key to making sense of everything else?

So, now we've hyperventilated together, take a minute or two for a deep breath, a soothing cuppa or, better yet, a Haagen Dazs. And prepare to roll back the curtains and look at some clues that this isn't all there is.

Chapter 2

DESIGNS ON YOU

Are there any clues to the 'God' question?

Can it really be, in the great scheme of things, each of us is no more significant than a boil on the backside of a baboon? When all is said and done, is that all there is?

When our clogs have been popped, our bucket kicked, and the daisies well and truly pushed up, have we done no more than make an infinitesimal contribution to the human gene pool? And have we been of no more consequence than what was once a hedgehog but is now only a faint blur in the middle of the road?

If there is no God then the answer in every case has to be 'yes'. But there is a vast amount of evidence to suggest a very different story.

The miracle of life

Imagine this. There you were enjoying a pampered existence in a safe and secure home – where life was constantly like those sleepy moments between dusk and dawn. The sounds reaching your little ears were always at a muffled minimum. Feeding was effortless and just an umbilical cord away.

Life was such bliss as you floated around in a human cargo

carrier. Then it happened – the big squeeze. An earthquake turned inside out. Moving lower all the time, you felt like toothpaste in the tube from hell. The push and shove from womb to world seemed an eternity. Then suddenly – pandemonium. It was all bright lights, cold air – and some crazy person swinging you upside down and slapping your backside.

But that was not your only welcome. Somewhere there was a parent or two – reduced to jelly, their emotions a wreck. The sight of your little wrinkled body had induced an intoxicating cocktail of joy, gratitude and wonder that simply engulfed them.

Such is the miracle of life. Something which dramatically focuses our attention on something or someone greater than ourselves.

At least that's been my experience – five times. Maybe you've never witnessed a birth and can't quite remember your own. But indulge me for a moment, because I think what happens in the birthing room provides a large clue towards answering the God question.

The fact of life

What is it that can so capture our attention? First there is the sheer miracle of life itself.

I will never forget the birth of our first son. Not because a blackbird flew in and began swooping round the delivery room. Or because of the initial panic when his first breath took so long to happen. But because I knew, overwhelmingly, he represented something way outside the united contribution of my wife and myself.

We had done our bit but were only too aware that we did not – and could not – create life itself. For that, the credit and recognition was due elsewhere. So I stood there wearing a stupid surgical cap, holding a little miracle in my hands while the tears ran down my cheeks. It was a 'God moment', and I was so grateful I had someone bigger than myself to thank.

Above all else, it was the creation of life itself that was so astounding. This new person was far more than the sum total of its DNA or the combined value of its chemical compounds. That's why, to lose a child is not an event in the same order as even losing everything we own. Can you compare losing a winning lottery ticket – even on roll-over week – with the loss of a child?

The loss of a child has nothing at all to do with the thought of wasting nine months of discomfort. Or 'having to go through all that again'. We treasure that new life because of what it represents if it stays – and because of what we lose if it goes.

Attention to detail

The second thing that captures our attention is the splendour of the packaging in which the new life is wrapped.

Eyes, hearing, reflexes, a motor mechanism that grips on an offered finger, a pre-programmed understanding of what food is and how to find it. The tiny heart that patters away. And those little lungs so capable, from the first moments after birth, of breathing air – and then hurling it past vocal chords to create such a voluminous blast of sound.

This bundle is mind-blowingly complex – made up of 60 trillion cells, with each cell carrying more information than could be stored on the shelves of a university library. And it is also stunningly unique – with a never-to-be repeated blend of 6,000,000,000 distinct, separate and precise instructions – that make up its genetic code.

To underscore the point, I was tempted to unpack for you the astounding complexity of just one organ – the eye. But I took pity on you. The simplest description I could find as to how light becomes sight ran to six hundred and twenty-three closely typed and complex words. And it was festooned with everyday jargon like picoseconds, transducinrhodopsin, and phosphodiesterase.

But the heart of the message was clear. The eye alone is so complex a mechanism – involving intricate chemical actions and minutely timed and accurate reactions – that the concept of it being no more than an accident stretches belief.

Not that new parents tend to be obsessed with physiological details when caught up in the wonder of the moment. Their comments are more likely to be limited to 'ooh', 'ah' and 'just look at those dinky little fingers'. But the message is the same. Such a miracle of design and perfection turns our hearts and minds – however briefly – to the someone who made it all possible.

A world of design

The created wonder of that new-born child is but a speck in an equally complex universe. If the new parent takes a moment to look past their reflection in the window, outside to the night sky, their sense of awe can only increase.

This is another clue that there's somebody out there. Just like that tiny baby's body, so our planet, and our solar system, our galaxy, even beyond to the universe – all of it is infused not with randomness but with intricate and finely balanced design.

Try this for size:

- If the ratio of protons to neutrons in creation were to change by more than one part in only 100,000,000,000,000,000,000,000,000,000,000,000 – galaxies and stars would not hold together.
- If the force of electromagnetism were slightly stronger or weaker, atoms would not be able to hold electrons properly and the necessary molecules for life would not exist.

- If there were the slightest variation in the velocity of light up or down, life would be impossible in the universe. You and I wouldn't be here and nor would anyone else.

Does that all strike you as something a little more than a piece of good luck? Random chance?

Instead of numbers, let me try you with a 'picture'. The first computer I ever bought came with a remarkable little programme called 'Orbits'. It traces the complex and consistent relationship between the orbits of the planets in our solar system.

All I do is click on any two planets on the list provided and hit 'go'. Within seconds a stunningly beautiful pattern – based on the constantly changing gravitational pull between the two – fills the screen. The effect is much like the Spirograph drawings of a past generation. Or a highly complex piece of lace filigree.

In this way it expresses the finely tuned design and balance of our universe. If either the shape of the orbits or the speed at which the planets travel are changed by as little as 1/1000th the end result would be not a beautiful pattern but a screen filled with what looks like a scribbled mess.

All this design points to one obvious conclusion – a designer.

It makes sense. The beautifully created St Paul's Cathedral didn't just appear in London one day. It gained the benefit of having had a gifted architect in the person of Sir Christopher Wren. This is equally true of the lovely Ferrari 355 F1 Spider. The awesome design both in body and engine had a whole team of technicians and planners behind it.

In other words, it is unthinkable to have design without a designer. And this is not just a layperson's view. Note the verdict of those from the scientific community:

- Astrophysicist Paul Davies wrote, 'The laws of physics seem themselves to be the product of exceedingly ingenious design. The universe must have a purpose.'

- Albert Einstein argued that (General Relativity causes) 'the necessity for a beginning and the presence of a superior reasoning power'.

- Scientist Stan Osterbauer wrote, 'The physics of the universe and the intricate design of nature compel me to conclude that there must be an ultimate designer.'

- Astronomer George Greenstein wrote, 'Is it possible that, suddenly without intending to, we have stumbled upon scientific proof of the existence of a Supreme Being?'

The existence of our emotions

It is not only the things we can see and touch that point us to the likelihood of there being a God. The same is true of our feelings.

So how are you feeling? Happy? Sad? Hopeful? Angry? Do you appreciate beauty? Do you react against injustice or the exploitation of others? Our ability to feel such emotions is a further clue to there being more to life than this.

Think it through. If we are nothing more than the result of endless random mutations – with the survivors being those best equipped to do so – where do emotions or conscience come from? They're not essential for our survival. In fact, feelings of pity and concern for justice put our future at risk – as they can lead to acts of self-sacrifice.

It has been suggested that our inbuilt sense of justice and fair play has nothing to do with a God who created us – that it comes from our social conditioning. The thinking is that everyone around us accepts these things and we have subconsciously bought into them also. If this is true, where did these concepts come from in the first place? How did a sufficient number of people initially hold to them strongly enough for us to be conditioned so well? And how come children are obsessed with 'it's not fair' long before they encounter the 'rules' of grown-up society?

This helps us realise we are not mere instinctive creatures – like dogs or cows. Two dogs don't enjoy a spaghetti while watching the sun go down – except in a Disney film. Cows don't stand back to admire the craftsmanship and quality of the new milking machine.

Could you imagine Hitler's dog joining the Allies on a matter of principle? Or Toto leaving the set of *The Wizard of Oz* because the dog regarded Judy Garland's performance as under par?

Our sense that there is a God

Anthropologists know it. Archaeologists know it. Palaeontologists know it. From the very beginning of human history people have always and intrinsically believed there is a Supreme Being. When ancient burial sites are excavated – along with the club, bronze arrow, or spear – there is usually some sort of idol or object which points to the deceased having believed in some sort of over-arching deity or God.

We just can't help it. It is part of the very stuff we are made of – this deep, natural subconscious belief in a power or person bigger and greater than we are.

During the starkly atheistic days of the former Soviet Union there were those who came to believe there must be a God on the basis that the authorities were so concerned to tell them there wasn't one. Their logic was simple: if there is no God there would be no need to tell us.

How wise they were. There has never been a campaign to deny the existence of the tooth fairy, or Father Christmas –

we know they are not real. And there has never been a time when the prevailing view of society is that there is no God – which is a huge pointer to the probability that there is one.

Even the very fact our reflexes lead us to call out to God in our time of need – or shout abuse at him in times of disaster – underlines the likelihood of his very existence.

What could this God be like?

Before we go any further, I'd like permission to briefly blow your mind. Let's step back – way back – and consider some thoughts on the greatness of God.

We humans assume God is just like us only somewhat bigger – and older. We imagine his mind is much like ours – as are his feelings and actions. But that can't possibly be true. God can't be anything like us. He simply has to be far greater in every way – and vastly different from us. Let me explain.

God is bigger than space

Our simple logic tells us that design requires a designer, matter requires a maker, and motion requires an initiator. Therefore, in the beginning there could have been nothing but God – and then he rolled up his celestial sleeves and got to work. Interestingly, this is exactly the way the well-known opening of the Bible tells it, 'In the beginning God created the heavens and the earth.'

What could that mean? Please lend me your imagination for a moment.

Imagine this very page you are looking at represents the universe – and God is there too. All the letters on the page are the stars and planets. So where do you picture God? Somewhere, mixed in the middle of the universe with all these letters perhaps? Maybe he's hiding behind planet

Pluto? But that cannot be. God isn't 'mixed in'. For God to be truly God he cannot be confined to space – something he has created.

So let's start again. Now, imagine this page as blank – before any words were placed on it. In the beginning there was only God – he is the page. Then he created. Where did he put his handiwork? Here, on the page, *within* himself.

You see, in the beginning God had to create a space – a place to locate the universe. The only place he could put stars, planets, and all he created was inside of himself. Which means, no matter how vast and immeasurable the cosmos may be, God can only be even greater.

God is greater than time

Before God began to create there was nothing – not even time itself. No days, hours, minutes, seconds and so on. Instead of 'time' there was 'eternity'.

What do I mean by eternity? Most people think of eternity, or 'for ever' as a lot of long chunks of time joined together. Not so. Time has limits and boundaries, starts and finishes, beginnings and endings, just like the bone in your forearm. Time, like everything else, had to be created.

But eternity is of a different dimension. It is more like 'super putty' or 'flubber' – stretchy and expanding. Eternity has no beginning and no end. Just like a page that has no edges – it keeps on going and going with everything God created laid on top of it.

So let's go back to the page again and the use of your imagination. If God is this page and the letters and words represent his creation, how can you illustrate 'time'? The answer is to draw a line, with a starting point and ending point, on the page. That would be time.

And God will still be greater than the print contained on the page and the line drawn across it. Scientists tell us the universe is 10 billion years old; some say 20 billion years, some are still counting. Light travels at 186,000 miles a second and so it has taken billions of years for us to see all the trillions of stars and millions of galaxies that are out there. And God is bigger and greater than all of it.

God is interested in the smallest detail

As we begin to understand the vastness of God and the sheer size he is, compared to us, it would be easy to despair. 'If God is so big,' you may be thinking, 'then certainly he has more important things on his mind than me.'

Of course not. God can not only be seen and known in the grand scale of the universe, but also in the micro scale of the atom. And even in 'little old you'.

The utter complexity of design and individuality even in the smallest details of our world suggests God's interest. To know that every snowflake in a blizzard is different – every fingerprint in a crowd of 12 million commuters is distinct – these little marvels of constitution demonstrate the interest of the creator.

Remember that baby we started out with? Such intricate design. Remember all those DNA particles – the chromosomes and cells, the atoms and all those little bits and pieces? They are like tiny little universes in their own right.

One of my highlights at Disney World, besides being mistaken for Goofy, was a ride at the Epcot Centre where we were miniaturised and 'injected' into the human body. It was an amazing adventure, where we were attacked by white blood cells, sucked through the chambers of the heart, breathed past tiny fibres in the lungs, and then the ultimate – we were electrocuted by tiny electron charges in the brain's neurons and shot back out into 'our own world' again.

How many different alternative universes there are all around us that we never notice. But do you think the ant or the worm escapes God's eye? Not if he made them. He understands vertebrates, invertebrates and even little blind fish down at the very bottom of the ocean. If 'Honey, I shrunk the kids' were possible and we fell through the soil into some alien-looking termite hole, God would even be there too. If God made it in such incredible detail, how can he not care about it?

God is not only God of the macrocosm. For him to be God he must also be God of the microcosm. He cares about the universe as it is, set within himself, both large and small.

A God who will never exhaust our exploration

Have you seen those Hubble space pictures? Stars, supernova and galaxy upon galaxy – swirling around so far away our minds cannot grasp what we are seeing. There is a universe where no man has gone before – but desperately longs to do so. We are interested in seeing it, experiencing it, travelling through it, and – ultimately – in inhabiting it. Why? Because we have an insatiable desire to discover and experience more of all that surrounds us.

Imagine what it would be like if you knew everything there is to know. Nothing else at all was left to learn, discover or experience. How boring, frustrating and pointless life would seem. You would probably top yourself.

But scientists tell us the universe is not static but ever-expanding – at an incredible rate. There will always be more for us to learn and experience. And yet, it is easily contained within an 'eternal' God.

The mind-stretching thing is this – if it is possible to know this eternally big God it would still take forever to do so. And that's not bad news – it's good news. Imagine, always finding something new, always discovering just that much more. And I don't mean book knowledge. I mean like falling in love over and over and over again – except with the same special person. So that what we feel and experience always goes deeper and deeper. That's what getting to know God, the one who made you, could be like.

Interested in you

So why did God do it? Why did he create it all – large and small? Was he somewhat bored as he hung about in eternity – and just fancied some exercise? Or is there a greater plan – one in which the human race is centre stage?

There is an astounding contrast between humans and any other living species. Only human beings have expressed any desire or ability to reach out to a Creator. This means there is something unique about the relationship between God and his human creation.

Human parents know how they feel about the offspring from their loins. But how does the Creator God feel about us, who sprang from his? Or, more particularly, how does he feel about you?

Does he have the same desire for intimacy and friendship that a parent harbours for their child? Why not? A child that lacks a deep 'hugged by a loving embrace' relationship with a parent is missing their due. And – until we know God in the same way – could that be true of us?

If so, our whole life misses its meaning unless we relate to this eternal God in the way he intends.

If there is a God like this, nothing could be more important than knowing who he is, what he is like and what interest – if any – he has for us. To fail to do so would be like the man who lived by candle power while scraping the mud off his shoes each night on what he thought was scrap iron. If only he had known this 'useless junk' was a powerful generator, he could have had all the light and heat he ever dreamed of.

It would be like the man who took back his chain saw after a week protesting that it did not do what the maker claimed.

'A tree every ten minutes was the promise,' he complained. 'The first day I only managed two. The next day I tried harder and managed four. Yesterday I pushed it to five. But I'm not happy.'

Timidly the sales assistant ventured the question, 'Could there be something wrong with the motor?'

'Motor? What motor?' the man replied. 'You mean there's a switch to give it power?'

I hope I have switched you on. Because if God is there, creating a living relationship with him must be as important as breathing itself.

Chapter 3

SECRET SPIDERS

Who knows enough to say for certain?

Despite all the clues to something or someone bigger than ourselves, perhaps you still have honest doubts. You have heard the talk of design, purpose, inner conviction and the rest, but continue to see such belief as wishful thinking or childish delusion.

Your vote may remain with those who simply can't bring themselves to believe in a higher or greater power. With them you say something like, 'As humankind grows to maturity it needs to shed such an outmoded belief – in much the same way as we no longer have any practical use for our appendix, guineas, and typewriters.'

Let's imagine this is the way you see things. You are an atheist – a word taken from the Greek and which roughly translates as 'no God'. In which case, please indulge me for a moment by answering a simple question. Out of all the vast knowledge existing in the universe, how much of it do you personally possess? In other words, how much do you reckon you know of all that can be known?

Five per cent? One per cent? 0.0001 per cent? The merest smidgen?

Now here's the rub – and a final question. Is it remotely

possible for God to exist somewhere in that vast area of knowledge that is not yet yours?

To put it another way, is there a spider in your room? At this moment, I assume you can't see one, hear one, see one, or smell one. But who would be so foolish as to say with absolute certainty, 'This room is sans-spider'? Because somewhere, outside your knowledge there may be a whole convention of them, just waiting to head for your bath.

To use examples from real life, who could believe in the existence of a stone that floats on water? But such a stone does exist. And who would countenance the existence of a furry animal with webbed feet and a bill which lays eggs like a duck but has fur and suckles its young? But such a creature is truly alive and well.

In the same way, could, just possibly, God exist beyond your present comprehension, understanding, knowledge and experience?

Say 'yes' and you are no longer an atheist but an agnostic – a small but significant step forward.

The word 'agnostic' comes from the Greek word for knowledge and simply means 'not knowing'. It's a very honourable word, even though it's rather gone out of fashion – much like the word 'spiffing'.

It's highly respectable to own up to not knowing whether there is or isn't a God. But only if you're the right kind of agnostic – because there are two very different sorts. There are 'ornery' agnostics and 'ordinary' agnostics.

The ornery agnostic says, 'Not only do I not know if there is a God, neither do you or anyone. And nor will you, now or for ever and ever.' Making sure there is no 'Amen' slipped in at the end. In contrast, the ordinary agnostic says, 'I don't know – but I'm wide open to knowing, should the right information come my way.'

If you're the former then goodbye and goodnight. There is

nowhere for us to go from here. Your mind's set, closed and that's that. However, if you're the latter, the following pages represent the most incredible journey you can imagine. But first we have to face an overwhelming problem.

The problem of discovering what God is like

So here you are, impressed by the clues and open-minded enough to dig a little further. You're ready to find answers to the big question, 'What exactly could this God be like?' And it's at this point you hit the buffers because there is no way you or anyone else – left to their own devices – can find out.

We may be able to establish some general principles but to take things any further is beyond us. Does that come as a shock? I'll do my best to explain.

Think through some of the key questions that need answers so far as the God agenda is concerned.

- Are we talking about a force or a personality? He, she or it?
- If this God is/has a personality, what values and feelings does 'he' have – indifference, kindness, goodness, revenge? Or what?
- What are his plans, purposes and expectations of the planet and its people – including us personally?
- Does he have mood swings?
- Is he one of many – or one without equal?
- Does he take it out on people who don't toe the line – or turn a blind eye?
- Has this God, having set everything in motion, retreated to a safe distance to watch how it all turns out – like pre-programming a washing machine?
- Or does God involve 'himself' in the day-by-day moment-by-moment affairs of all that has been created?

These are big questions. The temptation is to believe that all it will take is a little logic and some stirring of the grey matter for the answers to pop into place. Please think again – because there are some solid reasons why trying to use our own mental capacity to crack the God code will land us in the theological soup. These same reasons also help explain why so many people have such varied ideas as to what God is like.

There is a limit to our knowledge

We have yet to find a cure for the common cold. So how can we possibly believe we know enough to discover the answers to the huge God-shaped questions?

If you have never tasted paw-paw how can you describe the taste? If you have never heard 'Love Is All Around' played backwards on a kazoo, how can you explain the sound?

If you don't have a degree in computer engineering, how can you tell me why my PC does the frustrating things it does? Or, without a PhD in microbiology how can you tell me what it is my mother-in-law baked me for my birthday?

The problem of the limit of human knowledge is perfectly displayed in the person of Christopher Columbus, who 'discovered' America. The reason the Native Americans were called Red Indians is down to him. Sploshing ashore on the beach dear old Chris was utterly convinced he'd arrived in India. The natives were probably too polite to tell him he was a tad out in his calculations. This is no big deal if you're only out searching for continents. But when checking out the Deity it becomes a more serious matter.

The story is told of four blind brothers who were given the task of describing an elephant – an animal outside the previous experience of them all.

Said the first, feeling its tail, 'It's like a rope.'

Said the second, feeling its body, 'No, it's like a wall.'

Said the third, feeling its trunk, 'No, it's like a snake.'

Said the fourth, feeling a leg, 'No, it's like a tree.'

The problem we face, like those four blind brothers, is that the God we are inquiring about is vastly bigger than our sphere of knowledge. He is therefore beyond our ability to discover what he is really like, except in a groping, inadequate way.

There is a limit to our reasoning power

A child asks 'Why?' and 'How?' and 'Why?' again – and again. The parent has the answers and would love to be able to give them. But the child's reasoning ability does not stretch far enough – to say the least.

That's how it is when exploring the God agenda. Our brain power does not match the task.

It's like trying to compete in the Le Mans 24-hour race in a 850cc Uno. Or trying to illuminate Wembley Arena with a 60 watt bulb. It's like asking the average six-year-old to grasp the intricacies of algebraic trigonometry. Only worse.

In terms of our ability to wrap our minds round all that God entails, we are as sharp as marbles. Indeed, we have about as much to offer as the woman from the American state of Arkansas who had been sitting in her parked car, with her hands clasped behind her head, for over two hours. At the beginning she had appeared to be asleep but finally her eyes were open and she looked somewhat strange.

Help was at hand when a concerned observer knocked on the glass to ask, 'Are you OK?'

The woman answered, 'I've been shot in the head, and I am holding my brains in.'

The ambulance service came rushing, to make the surprising discovery that the woman was fit and well – but had thick white stuff on the back of her head and in her hands. Investigation revealed the full story.

The heat in the car had caused a canister of ready-to-cook bread dough to explode. And, with the noise of a gunshot, the contents hit her in the head. The woman had reached back to investigate. On feeling the dough, she became convinced it was her brains. And passed out from fright while attempting to hold them in!

We may hold human intellect in high esteem – or to the back of our heads with our hands. But we are simply not able to comprehend a God of such vastness and complexity through the use of human reason alone.

A God who can fit neatly within the scope of our limited understanding is bound to be a distortion of what is true and real.

There is a bias to our judgement

Have you ever been to the dentist for a check-up hoping against hope there was nothing wrong – even if potential disaster was lurking somewhere beneath the enamel? Or taken your car for its MOT inwardly pleading for an all clear, even though a more accurate verdict would have been, keep the clunker off the road?

In each case the priority was your short-term gain rather than the long-term truth. And when we go looking for the reality of what God is like we face the same problem. We would prefer to find only the things that would please us. We would rather know only truths that add to our comfort.

Our own self-interest drives us to limit our discoveries about God to those things which fit our comfort zones, mesh with our timetables and accommodate our priorities. And God may well not be like that at all.

Suppose what we found revealed something unpalatable

about ourselves or unwelcome about God? We would have no motivation to dig it out, even if our limited knowledge made it possible to do so.

In other words, our 'search' for God is going to be like the assessment of a house seller describing their property – rather than the verdict of the prospective purchaser's surveyor. Consciously or subconsciously, we are interested in focusing on what we want to find to be true rather than what may actually be the state of play.

The only answer – is for God to open the communication

So is there no hope? Are we doomed never to know what is true and real about this God for whom there are such compelling clues? Can we only add our own speculation to that of every other voice – and so add to the confusion?

Not at all. But if there is to be a solution to our problem it has to come through the initiative of this God himself. Let me illustrate what I mean.

Jaws 3 was a goldfish our family won at the fair. We loved him – or her. We were never sure if the little thing understood where the daily supply of flakes came from or how much simple pleasure he gave us.

There was also no way Jawsie could comprehend our world, how we thought of him, or the extent we wished him to stop intimidating Bruno – his black guppy bowl-mate.

The only way to put that right, had it been possible, was for one of us to actually become a goldfish, enter the plank-tonised world of our fishy friend and talk his language on his territory. There was just no other way he could get the message as to who we were, what we were like and what our hopes for him were.

In the same way, if there's to be any possibility of us discovering the vastness and wonder of God, there is only one way it can happen. This is by God taking the initiative to make himself known to us. Our only hope is for this great big God, bigger than time and space, bigger than the universe itself, to somehow enter our world. For him to become like one of us, speak our language, see life through our eyes, suffer as we suffer and to give us a visible demonstration of what is true and real about him.

Of course, the thought that God could show up in our world flies in the face of all human logic – as I realised during a remarkable holiday encounter.

With three companions I waited patiently for a seat in an over-crowded rooftop restaurant in a small Portuguese village. It was one of those nights when everyone had swarmed out to enjoy a perfect summer evening. The waiter's invitation came: 'You wait an hour or share with one nice man who is nearly finished.'

And so we found ourselves sharing a meal with Mr MENSA – Brains of the Universe. Our new companion – already significantly lubricated with the house red – turned out to be the Dean of a major American university. To say he had brainpower is an understatement – fluency in four languages and several graduate degrees all sheltered beneath his high-domed and suntanned brow.

Our group sat mesmerised as our new friend, Dan, escorted us on a tour of his vast knowledge of human thought and wisdom so far as God and all things deistic were concerned. And then came the moment when it went threateningly quiet – as he condescended to ask what I believed and how it fit into the picture.

Time froze. It felt like the recurring dream of being caught in the supermarket in only an underlength tee shirt. 'Me?' I quavered – wondering how foolish I was about to sound.

But then I heard myself saying, 'Everything you've said sounds like humankind looking for God. But I believe God came searching for us.' And metaphorically tugged the tee shirt a little lower, while waiting for the anticipated verbal pat on the head from an academic twenty years my senior. It didn't come.

'Wow. That's absolutely fantastic. I've never heard anything like it before. So deep,' came the explosive and unexpected response.

So began an intriguing friendship, in which Dan afforded me the status of genius. Together the four of us explored the coast, while I helped this massive intellect understand that even a turbo-brain with twin exhausts and an overhead camshaft is not up to figuring out God for himself.

But isn't it beyond belief to even dream that the creator of the whole shebang would visit our world as one of us? Nevertheless, this is exactly what has happened.

God came into our world

At a given point in human history God left the timelessness of eternity and vastness of the universe and beyond to enter our world. He did so in the person of Jesus Christ some 2000 years ago. And the life he lived made such a unique impact that the calendars of history are now dated from his birth.

The best that most people can expect after they die is to have a road, an airport, or a stadium named after them. But the life of Jesus is such a landmark in history, every time we now read, say or write the date we acknowledge his birth.

Of the fact that Jesus lived there can be no doubt. There is too much evidence from the historians of his day to reach any other conclusion. I am thinking of writers like Tacitus, Suetonius and Pliny. And the best-known of them all, Josephus, a Jewish historian who lived in Rome and died about AD 100.

Not all those who recorded Jesus' existence were his

followers or agreed with what he did or said. But they did all accept that he lived. Indeed, although Josephus speaks dismissively of Jesus as 'the so-called Messiah', he records his life, his death by crucifixion and that 'on the third day he appeared to them restored to life'.

The fact that Jesus lived is a matter of record. The rest, as they say, is history.

God spoke our language

In Jesus, God took the initiative to make the details of his character and intentions of his heart known to those he had created. To do this:

- He was born to ordinary working people in a humble town in an insignificant Mediterranean country.
- He identified in every way with those he had created – even down to being born as a racial minority, experiencing life as a refugee and living in an occupied land.
- He passed up any special treatment for himself in the way of palace or privilege and so truly became one of us.
- He felt pain, hunger, tiredness, disappointment and betrayal.
- He took up the cause of the outcast and lonely, the misunderstood and under-privileged while being misunderstood himself.

Of course, it's some claim to assert that this Jesus was actually God. Couldn't we settle for him being just a super-charged version of Gandhi, Florence Nightingale, Bob Geldof and Uri Geller all rolled into one – a kind of humanitarian, wise, wonder-working magician?

We are about to face that very question.

Chapter 4

WHO'S WHO?

Just another Gandhi or Mother Teresa?

Whatever your opinion about Jesus, one thing is certain. His life has affected history more than any other person who ever breathed the air on planet earth. So much so we've even set our calendars by the date of his birth.

Two thousand years after his birth you can surf the Internet for the name 'Jesus' and find more than two million pages which refer to him. One film of his life, called *Jesus,* has been translated into 500 languages and seen by more than 1.3 billion people worldwide. And one in three people on earth claim to follow him.

Jesus has inspired more works of art, more social reform, more compassionate action and more quests for justice than anyone else in history – by far.

Yet he came from an obscure backwoods town in a small enemy-occupied Mediterranean country. He lacked extensive education, never wrote a book or mixed with the rich and influential. Apart from a brief time as an infant refugee, he never travelled more than sixty miles from where he was born.

It's hard to wrap your mind round all that – but at least it's believable. What's hard to believe is the main reason for him making such an impact – that he was no mere mortal but God in human flesh.

And I don't mean God as in 'Eric Clapton is God'. But that this son of a Jewish carpenter was the creator of the universe who lived with his creation as a real card-carrying member of the human race.

If that claim has holes then millions of people – living and dead – stand condemned of the greatest act of sheer stupidity in the history of the planet. But if Jesus was, in fact, God in our midst no other historical event touches it.

So are we talking about wishful thinking or can we find evidence that might convince a sound mind like yours in the way it has mine?

What can support such a claim?

If someone landed on my doorstep saying they were my long-lost cousin – and expecting to be treated as such – I'd want something more than words to back up their claim. The same goes for Jesus and his extraordinary declaration to be God.

While the word 'God' may be at the top of his Curriculum Vitae, are there any points further down the page to help us believe the unthinkable could be true? Let me suggest a few.

His unique power and authority

Just as you would expect if Jesus were truly God, he did things humans don't do. To be specific – miracles.

Yes, I know we normal creatures have done some head-spinning stuff. I've seen the shows where David Copperfield and others make tall buildings disappear, turn tigers into Claudia Schiffer, produce people out of top hats and cut rabbits in half. But we know it's a trick. Somewhere there's a trap door, a mirror or an accomplice.

The things Jesus did were altogether different. And despite

modern-day protests that they were fiction, such claims were never made at the time.

Up which sleeve did Jesus keep 120 gallons of wine? And where did the water it replaced go? Or, if Jesus just used sleight of hand and a little colouring agent, how come the guests at the wedding where it happened gave it four stars?

In which false compartment did Jesus keep enough bread and fish to feed more than 5,000 people? And how did he lay on a special effects department to switch off howling gales and torrential rain at the word of his command while on a journey by boat across a lake?

How did he heal the sickness and crippling conditions of multitudes of people while under the closest scrutiny of those who had known the sufferers for years? These observers could testify, for example, the man who could now walk had been on his bed for thirty-eight years. And the man who could now see had been blind from the day of his birth.

How did he bring back to life someone who had been dead long enough for his body to begin to decay? And how did he walk on water and get someone else to step out of the boat and do so too? And how did he . . . . The list is endless.

How? If he was God it would be a piece of cake – and quite a lot of loaves and fish.

His teaching focused on himself

If Jesus was God you would expect what he had to say to be utterly different from others who spoke about spiritual reality – and it was.

Jesus was the subject of his own teaching. It wasn't his words or example he pointed people to – but who he was. Other religious leaders directed people's attention to a code of practice or a supreme being. But almost every time Jesus opened his mouth, he spoke about himself.

In a mere human, that would put him in the same category as the egomaniac who hijacks every conversation to talk endlessly about himself. You've met them – and don't like them. Jesus was different.

But if Jesus were God nothing could be more genuinely important than explaining himself. And he would be able to do so without getting up our noses.

He was all we could hope a God would be

If God walked the earth, what would you want him to be like? And to what extent does Jesus match it? Let me try a few examples on you – just a smattering of all that could be listed if there were time and space to do so.

Jesus was compassionate. Faced with a widowed mother whose only son – and her sole means of support – had died, Jesus raised him to life. Face-to-face with lepers, the AIDS victims of the day, he did the unthinkable and touched them.

Jesus left no one out. Prostitutes, people who lived on the edge of society, social outcasts were all welcomed by him. And women, the underclass of the day, received special affirmation and dignity from the way he treated them.

Jesus made ordinary people feel comfortable in his presence. There was nothing super-religious or stand-offish about him. Children swarmed round his feet, he was a welcome guest at a wedding, he enjoyed a normal social life.

Jesus detested religious hypocrisy. He spoke out against those with a better-than-thou attitude. Religion for the show of it stuck in his throat – and he said so.

Jesus welcomed those ready for a new start. He never wrote
people off. A prostitute, a thief and collaborator with the
occupying enemy for example all received the chance to start
again. His life expressed all you hoped God would be like. No
one was too far gone for him to love them.

What did his friends think?

Those closest to us know the truth about us. For example, I
can look the bee's knees to those who hear me speak in
public – which I do quite often. On a platform, telling people
right from wrong and helping them find a workable faith for
themselves, I can come over as a cross between Mother
Teresa and the Angel Gabriel. For the truth, ask my family.
But please don't.

My family know how far short of my public image I come.
I'll spare you the details – and I hope they will too. But you
get the point. They know the truth.

That's how it was for Jesus. Which is why the opinions of
those who knew him inside out, on and off duty really count.
And their verdict – having spent three years listening, watching
and evaluating? To a person they came to regard him as God –
and went on to give their lives for what they knew to be true.

One of them, Thomas, actually knelt at Jesus' feet and
said, 'My Lord and my God.' Did Jesus respond with 'Get
up, man, I'm nobody's God!' No – instead he freely allowed
Thomas to worship him.

Those who knew Jesus well were united in their conviction.
Jesus was God.

Jesus made it clear he was God

But you don't only need to make your mind up based on the
evidence. You can also take Jesus' own word for it. That's

because in a full on, watch-my-lips way, Jesus made it absolutely clear that he was God.

You may hear people who should know better say there is no record of Jesus actually saying in words of one syllable 'I am God'. And they are right – but they have missed the point.

The reason Jesus didn't use that particular description of himself was because, having said it so plainly in other ways, it would have been wasted words. Let me explain what I mean.

There you are at the side of the road with smoke wafting from your car's engine. You have phoned your emergency rescue service – let's imagine it's the AA – and are waiting for the promised help.

A call on your cell phone announces deliverance is ten minutes away. And right on cue there appears a familiar yellow van, with the letters AA emblazoned on the sides and a flashing yellow light on top. A man gets out dressed head to foot in the AA uniform, clutching a tool box and a clipboard. Ten minutes later you are on your way, smiling with relief.

When you arrive home someone asks, 'Was the man who fixed your car from the AA?' And you reply, 'He didn't say.'

Of course he didn't. There was no need. And the same was true for Jesus. Everything about him was equally as clear.

So what were the 'messages' Jesus sent out that were the equivalent of our mythical road-side rescuer's?

He said he and God were the same

Jesus made statements like 'Anyone who has seen me has seen the Father'[1] and 'I and the Father are one'.[2]

He also said that to receive him was the same as receiving God; to welcome him was to welcome God.[3]

He spoke of having always existed

When the ancient Jewish leader Moses came face to burning bush with God in the desert, God gave his name as I AM to signify that he had always existed. And Jesus used exactly the same phrase when speaking to Jewish leaders telling them, 'Before Abraham was, I AM'.[4]

Heard through Jewish ears this claim to be God could not be more blatant than if Jesus had written the words 'I am God' in six-foot letters on the side of a house.

He forgave sin

To Jewish people, only God could forgive sins. So when Jesus told someone their sins were forgiven it was no different from saying 'I'm God'. And when he healed people of disease or disfigurement he was putting out the same message. Jewish people believed physical suffering was caused by the person's sin. For a person to be healed meant their sin had been dealt with – and only God could do that.

For example, when a paralysed man was brought to him, the first thing Jesus said was 'Your sins are forgiven.' Then, to prove the point Jesus healed the man – who picked up the portable bed he'd been carried on and walked away.[5] In both ways his actions proclaimed his identity as boldly as the insignia on the car repairman's uniform.

Indeed, whenever Jesus healed sick people – and he did a lot of it – he sent out the same 'I'm God' message. This was blasphemy – a crime punishable by death. Which is why killing him was so high on the agenda of those who saw themselves as custodians of the truth.

He acknowledged the title 'Messiah' for himself

For centuries the Jewish people had been looking for 'Messiah' to come. The one who would overthrow their enemies and set up a new kingdom in which they could live as free people. This Messiah was referred to in the Old Testament as the 'Son of Man' – a title frequently used by Jesus about himself.

During Jesus' trial the Jewish High Priest asked him, 'Are you the Christ, the Son of the Blessed One?' Jesus answered, 'I am, and you will see the Son of Man sitting at the right hand of the Mighty One and coming on the clouds of heaven'.[6]

To non-Jewish ears the answer Jesus gave may not sound like a statement that he was God. But his questioner was left in no doubt that this reply – full of Jewish imagery – was a claim to be God. So much so that the High Priest ripped his clothes – not in temper but in the traditional response to blasphemy – and cried out, 'Why do we need any more witnesses? You have heard the blasphemy.'

In all these ways, those who heard Jesus through the lens of their Jewish culture knew with absolute certainty he was telling them he was God. But the issue for us is, can we believe him?

The Trilemma – one step worse than a dilemma

Jesus said he was God, he did those things you would expect him to do if he were God, and those who were the closest to him believed him. So where does that leave us? The answer is, on the horns of a trilemma. Because there are three distinct possibilities.

Someone who says they are God can be only one of three things. They are either a total fruitcake, a downright charlatan, or telling the truth. They're a lunatic, a liar, or truly the Lord God.

So, which is it?

Jesus the lunatic?

There is only one way to describe someone who sincerely believes they are God, have the authority to forgive sins, and will one day give away seats in Heaven. An utter nutter. What else?

It reminds me of the official visit to a psychiatric hospital made by the then Prime Minister, Margaret Thatcher. Introducing herself to one of the patients she said, 'Hello, I'm Margaret Thatcher.' Came the reply, 'Don't worry dear, you'll get over it. I was like that when I came in, but they cured me.'

Stark, staring, raving mad – and to be utterly pitied. That's the only conclusion to be made about someone who claims to be God and who isn't. We may feel sorry for them – and hope they get suitable treatment.

In which case, does that sound like Jesus to you? Do you see even a hint of someone out of touch with reality? Consider his poise and composure. Weigh up the quality of his life and relationships, the skill and insights of his arguments. Measure the sheer richness of all he said and did – and its life-enhancing impact throughout history.

Does that sound like the record of someone who went through life completely deluded?

Lunatic? Certainly not.

Liar?

If Jesus was sane and not God he can therefore only be a liar. But he would be more than that. Having taught so much about the need for honesty he would therefore also be a hypocrite. And, as he died for his lie, he would also be a fool.

Is it really possible that such insight, wisdom, compassion and love could come from the life of someone who was involved in such blatant deception? Could someone regarded as the greatest moral teacher in history really be such an immoral person? It just doesn't make sense.

And let's face it, people who are sane only lie to get something out of it – even if only to get themselves out of trouble. But what did Jesus have to gain from such a lie? Absolutely nothing – except crucifixion.

Liar? No thank you.

Lord God?

This leaves us with only one possibility – that Jesus was actually who he claimed to be – God, the Lord of all. This is not an easy conclusion, nor one we can fully understand, but it's the one which fits the data.

James Laurence, who spends his time helping people understand the Christian faith, told me of his experience before an unruly group of students trying to explain God to them. It had not gone as well as he had hoped. And then it got worse.

A mocking voice from the back challenged, 'Tell me, have you ever seen God?' That, figured the class, was going to settle it.

But James replied, 'I could have done, if I'd been born at the right time.'

And this is the incredible reality at the heart of the Christian faith. God stepped into first-century dust and dirt to make himself known. God is not hiding, he has made himself plain to see.

If you – like James – had been born at the right time, you could have shaken the hand of God, talked with him, questioned him, listened to him, watched him, laughed with him and cried with him. For Jesus is God in a human body.

In fact, this is the whole reason for his unique impact on

history. Jesus came both as God and man. The astounding things he said and did were not down to him being more clever than anyone else who ever lived, or more ambitious, more skilful or more talented. What set him apart was that he is God.

Chapter 5

HEADLINE NEWS

Chinese whispers or solid evidence?

To be absolutely honest with you, there is another possibility about the identity of Jesus. The choice may not be exclusively between his being a liar, a lunatic or the Lord God. Couldn't he have simply been a legend?

Robin Hood has been the subject of a host of books and films. But there's scant evidence he or any of his exploits ever graced the planet. And will future generations confuse Conan the Barbarian as a genuine figure of history in the same way? In this case, couldn't Jesus – and all we claim to know about him – be no more than a sophisticated fairy tale?

Perhaps Jewish religious fanatics needed a Messiah and invented him. Or the modest exploits of an ancient charismatic figure became exaggerated out of all proportion. Was he just a larger-than-life personality whose PR got out of hand?

First century spin doctors struck and everything spiralled into free-fall. As a result, the leader became a legend. The man who walked to Jerusalem became a hero who walked on water. The working-class son of Joseph and Mary became the awesome Son of God.

There is another way in which 'Jesus the Myth' could have

come into being. This is as a result of deliberate distortions by his followers – who saw themselves as having something to gain as a result. Or because they believed him to be God and wrote him up as doing the things they expected God to do.

Could any of these explanations make sense of the seemingly unbelievable claims made about Jesus? Did he really turn water into wine, heal all kinds of diseases and even bring dead people back to life? More than that, can we possibly ever know the answer to questions like these?

What you want to know is, if you were to take this on board, would you be dumping your brains and taking on the intellectual status of a flat-earther?

The good news is, it won't take me long to convince you otherwise. Because the answers are so clear and obvious. If you can manage to believe Julius Caesar died with a friend's knife in his back at the Senate House in Rome then this is an absolute cinch.

Reasons to be confident in the gospels

There are so many sound reasons to be sure what we know about Jesus is accurate.

It did not all happen in a corner

Never underestimate how great an impact Jesus made while he was here. In terms of the attention he received it would have been much like that created by Princess Diana.

The world of Jesus' day almost literally shook under his impact. Crowds flocked, news travelled, people talked. But he was so much more than headline news. Lives were dramatically changed, families transformed, relationships enriched, poor people cared for.

Thousands of people were involved at first hand. A large

group of people began to follow Jesus around, hanging on his every word. All of them knew exactly what he had said and done.

In other words, this was not something dreamed up in some back room without witnesses. Instead, it was a drama acted out by a whole community. It did not start as a rumour or tittle-tattle – but as a national event.

People told the stories

As a result of the impact Jesus made, people couldn't stop writing and talking about him. The things he said and did were so revolutionary, the people would have savoured every detail – repeating the stories over and over to themselves and to others.

Those who lived in Jesus' day had a remarkable ability for keeping an accurate record of their history alive through passing on stories round the meal table or fireside. With there being no newspapers and few books, events were told and re-told by word of mouth.

Storytelling was the television of the day. Without it people would lose track of their history and traditions. It was essential – making it possible for information to travel great distances both geographically and down the ages.

People did the same with the life of Jesus. And should a story-teller stray from the truth another eyewitness was on hand to keep them on track.

Their memories were sharp

Some who spent the most time with Jesus even memorised the stories he told and the teaching he gave. This was what followers of a Rabbi did in those days.

Ordinary people also had the ability to recall their own vivid experiences. Remember, they were not being asked what they had for breakfast twenty years ago. These were life-changing events that happened in the presence of many witnesses, who could each contribute to filling in the picture. In the same way that's true for us today, dramatic events became deeply ingrained in their memory.

Do you remember where and how you heard about the death of Princess Diana? I do – in wide-screen surround-sound detail. I may forget what I did last Tuesday, but not a momentous event like that. Jesus' followers saw a man whom everyone knew had been blind from birth, regain his sight. They heard teaching which made a direct cruise missile strike on their hearts. That's the type of thing they were asked to recall.

I can just hear them, every time they got together, going over what he'd said or done that day.

'Did you hear that? The story about the son who ran away – that was a killer!'

'Yes – remember the detail about him eating what was left over from the pigs? But hey, were you standing there later when he healed that woman? She just touched his cloak, and was as right as rain. She'd been to doctors for twelve years, she said, and they hadn't done a thing for her!'

They put pen to papyrus

Some took on the job of getting it all down in writing. They were either eyewitnesses themselves, as were Matthew and John, or those who could get their information from eye-witnesses, as did Mark and Luke.

This means what we now know as the *Gospels* – with their accounts of Jesus raising people to life or healing the sick – came from the pen of those who had either taken part in the events themselves or spoken to those who had.

Of course, this is why they could give such close attention to detail and mention people and places they could never have otherwise known about.

The writers were not daft

The writers and their informants were not ignorant peasants. They included a former civil servant, businessmen and a doctor. And they were sophisticated enough to eventually travel to most of the known world.

The writers believed truth mattered. Those who took on the task of telling the story of Jesus were committed to getting it right. To them, the words and deeds of Jesus were too important to be casual about. And they were so convinced as to the truth of what they wrote, they went on to give their lives for what they believed.

They didn't get it wrong

The accounts of what Jesus said and did were all nailed down far too quickly after the events for it to have become blown up into a myth. Those who earn their crust studying such things argue that the gospels were written during the lifetime of people who knew Jesus personally, and within 60 years of the events.

That is just too short a time for distortions to take place that turn a man into a God. Legends like that of King Arthur of Camelot took centuries to take shape.

Enemies were watching

All the while, watching from the wings, were the enemies of this mushrooming movement – ready to pounce on any distortion or exaggeration. What was recorded had to be accurate and to stay that way.

This is probably the greatest test of all. Legends can sometimes grow up in families. We allow each other to get away with a little embellishment here and there. But when you know your version of events is under the scrutiny of those who are just longing to catch you out, you make sure you get it right.

Lots of copies exist

With the first believers scattered far and wide as the result of being persecuted for what they believed, they needed to keep in touch with the great story. Very soon, hundreds of copies of the things Jesus said and did went into circulation.

These manuscripts have been copied carefully down through the centuries by people equally committed to preserving an accurate record. And when copies from different eras are compared they match time after time.

Abundant evidence

So many ancient copies of the writings about Jesus and the first Christians exist, the evidence for Jesus and the things he said and did is overwhelming. People happily accept that King Harold II died with an arrow through his eye at the Battle of Hastings, yet this is based on only a fraction of the evidence that exists for the life of Jesus.

People still believe

Millions of people have already reached the conclusion that the Gospels can be trusted. Some have done so simply on faith. Others have sifted the evidence with painstaking thoroughness.

Those who have believed after checking the facts carefully include some of the most eminent scientists, scholars, academics and thinkers of the day – with IQs the size of telephone numbers.

It works

Imagine if the Highway Code came from the printers with typographical errors that changed the meaning. Or if the instruction book of some household gadget was incorrectly translated from the original Korean – and you probably know what that's like. The result would be chaos.

In the same way, if the Gospels are no more than distortions or inventions, those who tried to apply them to their lives would be left high and dry. But the exact opposite is true.

Even two thousand years later, when what Jesus taught is put to the test, it works. Far from being a distortion of what was said, or the re-arranged memories of people long ago, it continues to have an impact.

Today – and for centuries past – people of every walk of life and of almost every language and nation have put the message of Jesus to the test and found it works. They have lived and died by it. They have discovered a fullness to life, real peace of mind and confidence in the ultimate future by taking the words of this book as true.

So why do people still doubt the Gospels?

There, I told you it would not take long. Yet you may wonder why, despite the impressive evidence for the record of the life of Jesus, you still hear people say some extraordinary things in order to dismiss it.

When you hear people casting doubts on the Gospels it is worth checking out who they are and where they are coming from. You will invariably find it's not historians who have trouble with the Gospel record. It tends to be theologians – those who make their living working out what God is like.

So far as most historians are concerned the Gospels stack up. In their eyes, diligent witnesses set it all out with care, archaeology supports what they wrote and we are inundated with good copies of the manuscripts to show they have not been meddled with during the passage of time.

Some theologians are less scientific. They have a pre-conceived idea as to what is allowed to happen in the universe and how God should behave. And when the historical record says something else they make their own judgement against the hard evidence. In their terms, the things written down are impossible so there must be another explanation. And the explanation they like is that it is not true.

This begs a simple but profound question: 'If God had come to earth as Jesus, lived among ordinary people, done extraordinary things, suffered a criminal's death and come to life three days later, what evidence would have been left behind?'

Disbelieving theologians say, 'I don't like the question!' Open-minded historians say, 'The Gospels, of course.'

The Gospels record events that may seem beyond belief. And we may find it hard to credit they happened, judged against what happens in the average shopping mall on a Monday morning. But the authentic nature of the gospel record means we can be absolutely confident that the version of Jesus' life found there can be trusted.

That includes the belief that history's most astounding event actually took place. Three days after he was certified dead, Jesus came alive again. And that's where we are going next.

Chapter 6

BOO!

No longer dead and buried?

Just when the authorities were uncorking the champers, convinced this upstart preacher was no more – he pops up again. Here, there, and everywhere! No longer dead and buried but walking, talking, and even eating – at least, he is according to his followers.

Having been thoroughly executed and hermetically sealed in a tomb, the word on the street is, Jesus is alive and in remarkably good health.

Beyond belief? Not to those who saw it with their own eyes. And not to the billions who have trusted their story ever since.

Can it really be true?

Historians see the resurrection of Jesus as one of the most authenticated events in ancient history. But in recent times others have thrown up a whole handful of theories to explain it away.

You'll have heard some of them, such as:

He never died. Jesus was not dead when they took him down

from the cross. He may have looked that way – but life still flickered within him.

And then, in the cool of the tomb, Jesus began to feel a lot better, dusted himself down and said 'Boo' to the world.

It was theft. The disciples of Jesus sneaked in and plundered the body right from under the noses of the guards.

Or perhaps the Jewish people or the Romans stole the body.

The wrong place. The mystery is all wrapped up in the disciples being dumb enough to turn up at the wrong tomb. Distraught with grief and confused with emotion, they simply turned left instead of right and got overly excited about another tomb that was empty.

All in the mind. The disciples were involved in a mass hallucination, say others. Or perhaps the disciples were only speaking 'figuratively' when they said they saw him.

Could any of these possibilities make sense of it all? It's easy to check. Hop on the Enterprise, hit warp factor seven and land at the time it was all happening. Did I say easy? The other way is to let the culture of the times and the eyewitness accounts recorded in the Gospels speak for themselves.

Was Jesus still alive when he left the cross?

What would the Roman soldier in charge of the execution crew at the time tell us?

Based on the way crucifixions were conducted and what the Gospel writers tell us, it would be something like: 'At a crucifixion it's my job to make sure they're dead – really sure. Only then will the officials release the body for burial. I've done hundreds of crucifixions – and never got it wrong. Wouldn't dare to.

'And we had to keep a special eye on this one. Any doubt he wasn't dead and I'd have done to him what I did to the two on either side of him – broke their legs so they choked on their own weight.[1]

'But I knew he'd had it. Especially when I whacked my spear into him and all that blood and stuff ran out. Was he dead? One hundred per cent. He couldn't have been anything else.'

Or let's let Joseph of Arimathea, the follower of Jesus who looked after the burial, have his say.

'Not dead? Woke up in the tomb and made his own way out? That has to be fantasy – because we followed Jewish burial customs to the letter.

'First we washed the body and dead bodies just feel different. Then wrapped it with linen grave clothes, starting at the feet and working upwards. Then we applied 75 pounds of aloe and myrrh – a thick and pungent gooey tree resin – which glued it all together.[2]

'We left, pulling out the wedge holding back a huge stone which then slipped into position to cover the opening. And the authorities sealed it and placed a security guard unit outside to keep troublemakers away.

'To escape, Jesus would have needed to rip his way out of 75 pounds of super-glued cloth, knock over a two-ton stone and make himself invisible to the highly trained guards.

'That's beyond belief!'

Was it a grave mistake?

What would Jesus' close friend Mary Magdalene tell us? She and another woman were the first to find the tomb empty.

'When I went there I didn't expect to see anything else other than Jesus' body. But here was the tomb – empty.

'I could only think that the officials had taken his body

away somewhere. But then Jesus himself came to me, called me by name and tried to calm me down.'[3]

Let's let Jesus' friend Peter take up the story:

'Mary's news sent me racing to the tomb. And I couldn't believe it! There was no body – only the heavy, sticky grave clothes – left behind by someone who was obviously very much alive.

'That's what first convinced us that he raised himself from the dead, passing through garments that weighed as much as three boxes of fish.[4]

'Did we go to the wrong tomb? You don't forget where you bury the most important person in your life. Anyway, how did the grave clothes get there if I went to the wrong place?'

Was it all in the mind?

Supposing the deeply bereaved followers didn't really see Jesus and, because they were so expecting him to rise from the dead, it became a wish fulfilment. But, if that were the case, would they have made it so impossible for the body to move – by using all that cloth and gunk to truss him up and weigh him down?

Let me illustrate. Your car has just had a very considerable altercation with a brick wall. Next stop is the scrap heap. You don't ever expect it to run again and so you behave accordingly – removing the plugs, points, wheels and a few other rattley bits.

But what if you have some wild hope that a fairy will rejuvenate the heap overnight and deliver it to your door in mint condition three days later? In that case you will play your part to help – by leaving the wreck as intact as possible. But you have no such expectation. And so you don't.

This is exactly the attitude the disciples showed to the body of Jesus – but with considerably more respect. And it tells us they had no expectation of a second act.

In which case, perhaps a few coincidences were blown up out of all proportion? Not at all.

What we are invited to believe is not based on a fleeting glimpse by a couple of people on a hot afternoon after a very liquid lunch. Nor is this about an isolated sighting of Adolf Hitler on a beach in some Central American city, or Elvis on a porch in Hawaii.

Or could it all have been an illusion?

There was nothing brief or casual about the contact the disciples had with the risen Jesus. Over a period of about forty days they couldn't stop bumping into him. It happened all over the place – on the road walking, in a private room, on top of a hill, by the side of a lake.

And these weren't quick two-minute 'How's your father' conversations. They talked and talked together – about the way the Jewish scriptures had foretold his life, about their own personal needs, and about his future plans for them.

Jesus appeared to a vast range of people who can't all have simply been overcome with emotion. Different types of people who had all kinds of reactions.

- At least ten people locked in a room together were terrified when the unexpected happened and Jesus appeared among them.[5]
- Cleopas and his friend on the Emmaus road were gobsmacked when the man who joined them turned out to be Jesus and started to share a meal with them.[6]
- Thomas will go down in history as 'the doubter', because he absolutely refused to believe until he met Jesus face to face. Jesus then invited him to touch the places on his hands where the nails had gone in.[7]

In each case Jesus took time to give those involved what they needed at the time – comfort, reassurance, explanation, physical evidence. And the details, which were recorded by the gospel writers, sound absolutely genuine. There's no ring of something churned out as the religious party line. Or of fanciful embellishment.

Did they die for a lie?

Maybe the followers of Jesus just made it all up. Somehow they managed to steal the body from under the noses of the Romans, buried him secretly, and began pumping out the 'He is risen!' message. And fame and fortune awaited.

But most of those early followers of Jesus met unpleasant deaths – inflicted because they believed Jesus was alive and kept on saying so. If they knew it was a lie they were among the most stupid people ever to have lived. For who is daft enough to give their life for a cause they know to be based on a lie?

Instead, the reality of the resurrection transformed their lives completely. I'm thinking about people like Peter, Paul and John.

- Peter, a hot-tempered fisherman, was once so scared of being arrested with Jesus he swore and lied his way out of trouble, denying he ever knew him. Belief in the resurrection made Peter a bold, outspoken leader of the early Christians. It's said he died by being crucified upside-down.
- Paul, a highly educated Jew, was once determined to wipe out all traces of those who believed. Then he came face to face with the resurrected Jesus. Soon he was travelling throughout the known world telling

people the news. Tradition tells us he was executed by the Roman Emporer Nero.

- John, Jesus' close friend, was also a fisherman and nick-named 'Son of Thunder' because of his quick temper. Through the impact of the resurrection he became a leader of the early Christians, and died in exile.

These are but an infinitesimal fraction of all who have risked life and limb for their belief in Christ and his resurrection – both then and now.

What transformed these ordinary people?

Think back to the scene where Jesus breathed his last. Huddled under the feet of their dying leader stood a rag-tag, discouraged bunch of wannabe's. It was all over but the burial. High hopes didn't pan out. It was great while it lasted. But now he's dead. Time to go back home, pick up the pieces and keep clear of all those who will say, 'I told you so.'

Yet only weeks later these very same people are out in the open, fit to busting, and telling all who will listen about the living Jesus raised from the dead by the power of God.

Something had so galvanized the followers of Jesus, that faith in him swept the length and breadth of the Roman empire in the next 300 years. What one single event could bring about such a transformation other than Jesus truly rising from the dead?

British journalist Mark Tully revisited the scene of Jesus' life interviewing people for a BBC TV series on Jesus. It ended with his own view. He said, 'That man was probably a failure in his own time . . . He taught in strange riddles. He didn't convince his fellow Jews. And he didn't overthrow Rome.

'From that failure I have come to what, for me, is the most important conclusion of all. That the hardest, apparently least historical article of Christian faith, the resurrection, must have happened. If there had been no miracle after Jesus' death, there would have been no grounds for faith in a failed life. No resurrection . . . no church.'

Dare we believe?

It's one thing for eyewitnesses to believe such a startling thing happened. But surely we can't be expected to. Yet why not? Throughout life we take actions on the basis of the words of those who have seen when we haven't.

I've just had the flat roof on the very top of my three-storey house re-surfaced at the cost of a small fortune. And all because I believed the testimony of the expert who climbed up to have a look. I didn't ask for a photograph, ten other witnesses or a section to be brought down for inspection.

The eyewitness had all the credentials of an honest man, offered a cast-iron guarantee, and had everything to lose if I found him to be taking me for a ride. And so I believed.

I wasn't around two thousand years ago to see the resurrected Jesus for myself. But along with millions of others I have taken the word of those who were. The evidence is simply too overwhelming to believe anything else.

Chapter 7

WHAT A BLUNDERFUL WORLD

How'd we get into this fine mess?

Gardens where weeds never grow. Streets where it's always safe to be. Communities where everyone lives in harmony. Does that sound great? Well, it's a picture of the way God intended things to be.

In such a world, nations would always be at peace – never butchering each other's young. Resources would always be shared – so no one need ever go hungry. And people would live the same way individually – with no grab and greed, no might is right, no me at the expense of you.

Children would not be dragged through family wars. The elderly would not be neglected. Employees would not be exploited. Property would not be stolen and vandalised. Drunks would not drive, children would not be molested and people of other races would not be victimised.

What a mind-bogglingly wonderful world it would be. And that was God's Plan A. Everything in the garden was to be lovely – smelling sweetly in the nostrils of its creator. But it went rancid.

We've done it our way

What went wrong? The answer is 'we did'. Let me tell you the story.

In its opening pages the Bible paints a vivid picture of humanity in a beautiful garden in the midst of the whole of creation. As God surveyed the scene he declared everything to be 'good'. And when God uses the word 'good' it needs to be translated 'perfect'. Not in a picky, every blade of grass neatly combed kind of way. But in a top quality, not a blemish, breathtakingly wonderful kind of way.

That is the way it was intended to be – for ever.

But the humans chose to do it their way. The opportunity for them to behave as though they were God was off limits. But they decided to trespass.

What happened next was like the gears of a car being crunched into reverse while speeding forward down an open highway. With a heart-tearing lurch, the whole of creation shook and splintered – never again to run as it was meant to.

For those who caused this catastrophe there was no longer a place in the garden. Their relationship with the creator was shattered. They now felt exposed and naked. And everything had been spoilt. From top to bottom and middle to outside. It has remained that way ever since.

Our blunderful world is all down to us. And the key word is 'sin'. Because that's what caused the mess and continues to do so.

The reality of sin

The word 'sin' is much misunderstood – bringing to mind wagging fingers and miserable killjoys. We picture the stern-faced lord of the manor turning away the unmarried waif with her new-born child. Back into the falling snow she must go, condemned never to darken the door again.

Yet 'sin' is the perfect word to describe what has gone wrong with ourselves, our world and our relationship with the Creator.

To sin is to refuse to live in the way God intended. It's as simple as that. And the evidence for its existence is everywhere.

We know that our own self-centredness inflicts sadness, pain and disappointment on others. We know how often we fall short of our own standards. And be thankful that modern technology excludes a machine capable of projecting our innermost thoughts onto a big screen for all to see.

There is a fatal flaw in the universe and – though it may not be popular to say so – we are it. It is all because of sin, of which four things are profoundly true.

Sin is the state we're in

Sin is not so much about a list of things we do but, first and foremost, a description of our human condition. Let me try to explain.

Have you ever found yourself in charge of a supermarket trolley that spent its time charging into stacks of food no matter how hard you tried to steer it? The symptoms of the problem can be seen in the dents made in people or produce. But it's the condition of the trolley that's the real problem.

In the same way, I have a son who shows all the signs of suffering from asthma. You'll see him using a little 'puffer' from time to time, or stopping to catch his breath. These are just two of the symptoms of his condition.

We all have a condition which has symptoms. The condition is to be a sinner – and the symptoms are the sinful acts we do. Just as the supermarket trolley by nature chooses to go its way and my son is by nature an asthmatic, we are by nature sinners.

Our basic attitude is to steadfastly choose to go our way rather than God's way. We habitually think of ourselves first and others last. And even some of the best things we do are designed more to make us feel better about who we are than to help others.

Sin is not making the grade

Because of our condition we can never match what God expects of us. Look at it this way. Do you ever remember going into a store to buy a new pair of shoes while feeling pretty good about the pair you were wearing at the time? And cringing when the pair you tried on made the old look so shabby you couldn't even bear to wear them home?

Having seen perfection, we discovered our previously perfectly acceptable shoes were not so perfect after all.

It is similar when we compare what we are inside to what God expects of us. Most of the time we feel pretty good about ourselves. In our eyes, compared with most people, we are 'pretty good, thank you'. And compared with some others God should be grateful to have us on his planet. We're OK.

But God has a different standard. It's a 'new shoes' standard. It's one to match who he is and what he created. It's the standard of absolute moral goodness, purity and perfection – and it's the standard we are measured against. Which means, in his eyes we are like damaged goods well past their sell-by date.

Of course, there's a lot in us that's commendable. But the need isn't simply to scrape away the top layer of gunk to get down to the real bright and shiny me.

Think of it as though God created us with the ability to play darts and hit the bull's eye every time. But now, we can't even hit the board – we're so off target there are holes all over the wall. And this is true in every area of our life when seen from God's perspective. We constantly fall short, fail to make the grade, and miss the mark.

Sin is breaking the rules

Like Little Red Riding Hood, we all have a given set of rules to go by. Hers were simple:

- Deliver the goods.
- Don't talk to wolves – or any other strangers.
- Be nice to Grandma.
- Get home safely.

Our rules are best expressed in the Ten Commandments – God's non-negotiables for life at its best. Most of us know them – things like, don't lie, don't steal, don't commit adultery. The problem is we treat the Ten Commandments as though they were ten suggestions – or as a range of options in an opinion poll. We are as effective in obeying as was the kid with the red hood on her journey to Grandma's house.

Like Red Riding Hood, we have a choice. We can do things the way God wants them done, or the way we want to do them.

Why does it matter? Because God's rules are not of the 'Keep off the grass and no ball games in the pool' variety. They are for the best interest of everyone and everything. When we break God's wise rules we damage our relationship with him, damage ourselves and hurt others.

Yet these are far more than rules. They are the very fibre of society and the universe. To break them is to betray the one who made us.

Sin is an enemy that's after us

The wolf from Little Red Riding Hood was an important part of her story – because of his enticement. And that is another aspect of what sin does to us – it entices.

Back in the first pages of the Bible is the story of two brothers. One named Cain – a farmer. The other named Abel – a shepherd.

And here's where the wolf comes in. Just before Cain murders his brother God warns him, 'Sin is crouching at your door. It desires to have you, but you must master it'.[1]

In this way sin is like a living thing – as a wolf, a beast, an enemy crouching at our doors waiting to pounce and consume us.

Little Red Riding Hood's behaviour sounds a lot like that described by the prophet Isaiah when he wrote, 'We are all like sheep who have gone astray. . . . We have each turned to our own way'.[2] We may have stamped our hooves and bleated 'shan't'. Or just wandered off enticed by seemingly better things. But in both cases, sin has equally serious consequences.

What sin does

Having looked at what sin is, we need to complete the picture by understanding what it is that sin does – to us, to others and to God himself.

Sin spoils

Sin impacts us – and our world – in the way that the Exxon Valdez oil tanker impacted the environment when it ran aground in the Prince William Sound off Alaska in 1989 – spilling some 232,000 barrels of oil from her hold.

Within hours a thick black sludge coated the snowy white coastline. And that was just the beginning. Three-quarters of the salmon population that normally migrates to the area did not return the following season. Thousands of otters were poisoned, and thousands of birds died. That illustrates what sin does to our relationships, our motives, our attitude and our actions. What should be pristine clean is utterly tainted.

Sin is like an oily thumbprint on a pure white wedding gown. That is all it takes to spoil everything.

Sin is like the two fleeting frames of a nude woman slipped into the Disney Corporation's children's classic *The Rescuers*. On the big screen the offence was invisible. On video – in freeze frame – there was every possibility it could be seen.

A small 'sin' had spoiled the whole thing. Disney recalled four million videos and took a hit for £30 million.

How small a smear of washing-up liquid needs to be left on your cup to make your coffee undrinkable? How much damage to a load of light washing can one very small red sock inflict? How many salmonella germs does it take to close a restaurant?

In the same way, sin has a devastating impact on our lives and our world, spoiling everything it touches. Without it, we would have a clean conscience, an unsullied reputation, and unbroken relationships.

Sin separates

We were created to know God and to enjoy his company. But sin has become a barrier between us.

Sin is the cloud between us and God. It's what separates us from experiencing the warmth of his love. The prophet Isaiah puts it like this: 'Your sins have separated you from your God; your sins have hidden his face from you'.[3] How come? Because like oil and water, God's purity and our sinfulness don't mix.

To grasp this you need to realise the extent to which God's radiant purity and perfection are far beyond our understanding.

This caught my attention when a friend described to me in

stunning detail the beauty of the Taj Mahal which he had just visited. It was breathtaking and far beyond anything I had imagined from the photographs I'd seen. And I would never have known without his animated eyewitness account.

God's purity is like that. It is utterly beyond our understanding.

Within all that God is, there is not a drop of deceit, bitterness, rancour, malice or unkindness. Instead, his whole essence is one of love and purity. Which is why our sin keeps us from him. It reminds me of the summer my deep freeze broke down and all the food was ruined. 'Keep the evidence,' instructed my insurance broker, 'in case it is needed to prove your claim.' Within days the food from our commercial-sized feed-a-family-of-seven freezer had become one seething, maggot-ridden, fly-infested offensive mess. I could not bear the sight, smell or sound of it. Even now the very thought of it makes me retch.

This is how our sin impacts God. Anything less than purity and perfection is a stench in his nostrils, an offence to his eyes and a strident discord to his ears. This is why the implication for us personally is that our sin, while it remains unforgiven, keeps us locked out of God's presence for ever.

God will judge

But why can't God be a little more understanding about our sin? Couldn't he turn a blind eye and lower the pass mark a little? Such thoughts show we haven't even begun to grasp the seriousness of the situation. He simply knows what's best for his world, including us.

Don't picture God as an over-eager traffic warden just itching to call in the clampers, as someone who is at his happiest when making people miserable. You will see in the following pages, the very opposite is true.

In reality, it could be said that sin is its own judge and reaps its own rewards. That this is the natural outcome when light meets darkness. The light always reveals what is true. Let me try to illustrate what I mean.

I was proud of our lawn. The bits worn thin by the children's paddling pool had grown back. At long last it was verge to verge green and splendid – except for just the occasional weed. Or so I thought.

A neighbour offered some of his spare 'Weed and Feed' and was soon depositing it across my treasured possession in a nifty dispenser on wheels. 'It can only look even better,' I told myself.

Within days the truth was revealed, as large brown dead patches spread everywhere across what I had believed was near perfection. Judgement day had come and the truth was out. What had looked so good to my untrained eye had been the right colour but the wrong substance. Moss, clover and some stuff with odd Latin names had withered under the impartial evaluation of something that knew the difference between grass and weeds.

That's how it will be when we stand before God – as each of us surely will one day. In the searching gaze of his perfect evaluation, what seems so OK to us will be revealed in all its shabbiness and poverty.

God is fair

There is much more to God than him being our judge.

Standing before a school assembly I asked the children to list the components of the perfect parent. Once 'rich' and 'generous' were out of the way they got to the serious stuff – like 'fair'. Then came my loaded question, 'Do you expect to be punished when you step out of line?' The reply was unanimous and loud – 'Oh no!!'

Then came loaded question number two. 'So if your

brother or sister beats up on you or breaks your things they should also go unpunished?' Dilemma and confusion struck.

They wanted a parent who is both fair and unfair at the same time. And it's the same with us. We want God to put an end to wrong – so long as his actions don't cramp our style or have personal implications. We want him to step in and take care of all the bad things that happen in this world, but at the same time to leave us alone to do whatever we want.

But if God is to be fair he must deal with sin – including ours.

So how can that happen? What could God possibly do that would make him both fair and forgiving at the same time? How can he act with justice while showing love and compassion? How can he get us back to the garden and to being his friend once more?

Chapter 8

CRIME OF PASSION

Executed? But wasn't he such a nice boy?

It took two billion dollars – and the combined efforts of
hundreds of environmental workers – many months to clean
up the mess left by the Exxon oil-spill disaster. But what of
the cost to clean up the pollution of all creation, caused by
the spillage of sin into our world?

The answer to this question lies in two pieces of wood laid
over one another to form a simple cross.

The cross as a symbol

Symbols are powerful communicators. Companies spend
tens of thousands of pounds creating, copyrighting, and
getting into public view an icon which represents their per-
sona. They want something that conveys the essence of who
they are.

For Nike it's the tick. Britain's New Labour Party have a
red rose. American Express uses the face of a Trojan. Those
who died in the wars have the help of a poppy. The message
is, 'Look at this. Think of us.'

If symbols are so important, how come the one most often
used by those who follow Jesus is a cross? Why go for an

image most people know is a blatant link to the bloody and barbaric death of Jesus?

Couldn't they find something more consumer-friendly? A bunch of loaves and fishes, a footprint on water, a hand patting a child's head, or a star in the sky? But not a cross. Who would buy into a product represented by a symbol of torture and slow, painful death? It's like a company today using a hangman's noose or an electric chair as their logo.

So what is it about a cross that makes it so central to everything the followers of Jesus believe and stand for? And what's it got to do with me?

The answer is simple. Today people wear crosses but 2000 years ago – crosses wore people. That included Jesus. It was his death on a cross that formed the focus of attention for his followers and explains to us the significance of why he came.

Understanding the death of Jesus – a criminal's execution – is central to grasping what he was about. You can see this from the way the four biographers of Jesus devoted a quarter of their pages to the final week of his life. During which time he was arrested, tried, condemned and executed.

Instead of trying to divert attention from such a dis-honourable end the writers seem to do all they can to draw attention to it.

But why? What was it about the death of Jesus that his followers wanted so much to keep in mind?

Why do people think he died?

There are many opinions about Jesus and his death. I've had said to me things like:

- Jesus died because people could not live with the truth he taught.

- Jesus was a revolutionary and got caught up in a plot to overthrow the Romans who were oppressing his people.
- Jesus was a wimp and as such was an easy target for the Romans to make an example of.
- Jesus was the victim of the greed of someone who betrayed him for money.

How tragic if any of these were true. Because – in every instance – Jesus would have died caught off guard and misunderstood, having failed to achieve what he wanted. A life so full of promise would have ended in defeat and even disgrace.

What was his crime?

Are any of these theories on the mark? Or are they all wrong? What was the real reason for the death of Jesus? After all, if he was such a good and kind person, why was he strung up like a common criminal? What crime could they lay at his door?

In the eyes of the Jewish religious leaders

So far as the Jewish leaders of the day were concerned, Jesus had committed the greatest crime in the book – blasphemy. He actually said he was God – both by his words and his actions.

His popularity didn't go down too well with them either. Enormous crowds flocked to see and hear him – sometimes 10,000 or more. He also had an aggravating habit of undermining their authority by flouting the picky rules they had accumulated down through the years – by doing things like healing people on the Sabbath, the Jewish holy day.

Then he added cream and sugar by telling them they were hypocrites. But ultimately, it was Jesus declaring himself as God that stuck in their throats.

In the eyes of the Roman authorities

The Romans were in control of Israel at the time, which meant the Jewish authorities had no power to punish Jesus themselves. For that, they had to turn to the Romans.

So, with the end justifying the means, Jewish leaders came up with a few more charges and some lying witnesses. Which is why Jesus found himself tried for a Jewish crime by a Roman court.

And, the governor, Pontius Pilate, sentenced him to death because of his own complacency and for the sake of peace and quiet – even though his own verdict was, 'I find no fault with this man'.[1]

What Jesus said about his death

In a remarkable way, Jesus had a very clear understanding about what was on the horizon for him and why it would happen.

It did not take him by surprise. Like a person told by the doctor, 'I'm sorry, you have only six months to live,' Jesus knew his death was coming and even what form it would take.

He was clear enough to be able to tell his close friends and followers that the authorities were going to kill him.[2] He even told them how he would die when he said to his followers, 'When I am lifted up from the world I will draw all people to myself'.[3]

It was for a specific purpose. Not only did Jesus know he would die, he knew why. He spoke of his death not being aimless, or down to misfortune, or as simply an occupational hazard. There was a specific intention behind it.

He told his followers, 'The reason I came to earth is so I

could give my life as a ransom for many people'.[4] What that means we will come to in a moment. For now it's enough to see that his death was not a random event caused by misfortune or occupational hazard, but – by his assessment – something he specifically came to do.

What Jesus did about his death

Jesus did nothing to stop the process that led to his death. He went willingly to face his executioners. No top legal team were summoned to his defence. No ducking and diving or taking the Fifth Amendment. No 'it depends what you mean by "God"' stuff to escape the charge of blasphemy. Instead:

- He told his followers, 'No one takes my life from me, but I willingly lay it down'.[5]
- He said that he could have called on angelic troops to rescue him, but he chose not to.[6]
- He silently soaked up blows and abuse from people, priests and soldiers.[7]
- When asked by the Roman governor Pilate to defend himself, Jesus remained silent – in spite of knowing that only Pilate could grant his freedom.[8]

The gospel writers go so far to tell us that, at the time of his death, 'He gave up his spirit'.[9] Jesus even decided the exact time he would release his spirit from his body. It was only to be at the moment when all that his death was intended to achieve had been accomplished

The identity of Jesus is the key

So Jesus was accused by Jewish leaders, prosecuted by a Roman Governor, and Roman soldiers literally nailed him to a cross. But who killed him? The answer is 'I did' – and so did you. Such a provocative statement can only make sense when we fully understand who Jesus was.

God's love in action

The significance of Jesus' death is ultimately all wrapped up in who he was and what he came to do.

Jesus didn't stumble onto the stage of history – the script had already been written with him as the central character. He was to be the kingpin of God's rescue plan. The one who would deliver us all from the consequences of our sin.

For hundreds of years such a deliverer had been promised through the Jewish scriptures. This was not by way of some 'Mystic Meg', fortune-telling, shot-in-the-dark predictions, but through clear statements recorded in the Bible centuries before Jesus was ever born.

These prophecies included specific details about the one who would come as the deliverer, such as:

- He would be born in Bethlehem[10]
- Of a virgin[11]
- He would be betrayed by a friend[12]
- And sold for thirty pieces of silver[13]
- He would be struck and spat on[14]
- While his hands and feet would be pierced[15]
- And so would his side[16]
- The soldiers would throw dice for his clothes[17]
- While never breaking a bone of his body[18]
- He would be buried in a rich man's grave[19]
- And would rise again from the dead[20]

Do you know what the odds would be for any one person fulfilling even any eight of the eleven prophecies listed above? It would be like hiring the largest stadium in the world and filling it to overflowing with sweet wrappers – of which all were red except just one which was white. Then blindfolding someone and asking them to draw out the white wrapper on their first attempt. That's how easy it is – and how clear it is that Jesus was the one.

Don't imagine that Jesus was just a sharp operator who manoeuvred things so these prophecies worked out for him, becoming a hero of history through his own cunning. To do that he would have to control where he was born and how he would die, stop his executioners breaking his bones while they broke those of the men dying with him, arrange for his followers to select his grave after he had died, and then raise himself from the dead.

What was the point of Jesus' death?

To understand what the death of Jesus meant involves understanding the picture of sacrifice, which had deep meaning for the Jewish people.

I realise our modern minds may be unnerved at the thought of animal sacrifice. If you feel that way, don't ever ask someone in the poultry business how that poor defenceless chicken ended up as a clean shrink-wrapped carcass ready for you to drop into your supermarket trolley.

The picture of sacrifice

At the time when Jesus was first beginning to teach and heal, his cousin John the Baptist pointed to him and said, 'Look, here is the Lamb of God who takes away the sin of the world'.[21]

The Jewish people listening knew exactly what John was getting at. Their religion was a sacrificial one. They sacrificed animals to show God their willingness to turn away from the wrongs they had done and make a fresh start with him. Let me explain how it worked.

The person who needed forgiveness would bring an animal without any defects to the priest. This was to die as a substitute for them. First their hands were placed on the animal's head as an act of transfer. The blamelessness of the animal was then understood to have been exchanged for their guilt.

With the penalty for sin being death – the animal's throat was then slit. And when it died it carried the sin away with it. Justice had been satisfied.

Here was a graphic picture of a life for life. The innocent was slain so the guilty could go free. Which was exactly what John the Baptist said Jesus came to do. Jesus was to be the Lamb, sacrificed for the sin of the whole world.

And that was what happened on the cross when Jesus died.

Jesus was God's once-for-all-time sacrifice

Sacrifice – with an animal, a priest, a knife and a sinner – was needed regularly to keep paying sin's price.

But Jesus' death was once and for always. When Jesus cried from the cross, 'It is finished'[22], it was. The God of the cosmos did what no animal sacrifice could ever do. He paid the price for the sin of the whole world. He fully and finally made one sacrifice – there on the cross.

This is the *ransom* I mentioned earlier. Sin has kidnapped us at gunpoint and left the message: 'Give me more money than you can ever get your hands on if you want your life back!'

'That's impossible!' you protest.

'I know,' says sin with a smirk.

And that's the problem.

The day the sun stopped shining

I'd like to help you grasp the immensity of the price Jesus paid to make our forgiveness possible. Picture the scene. You're there on that momentous day looking up at the cross. It's noon. Suddenly you can't even see Jesus. You can barely even make out the face of the person next to you. In the middle of the day it's gone as black as midnight.

Don't be surprised. More than 800 years before this incredible event a prophet named Amos predicted such a unique day in the future. He wrote, 'In that day, declares the Lord God, I will make the sun go down at noon and make the earth dark in broad daylight'.[23]

As you stand there the day foretold by Amos has finally come. What you are seeing will be written up by Luke in his Gospel, saying, 'It was now about the sixth hour (12 noon), and the darkness came over the whole land until the ninth hour (3pm), for the sun stopped shining'.[24]

The darkness showed God's curse

That darkness points to the magnitude of what is taking place. Despite all that Jesus physically suffered, there was a far greater pain in the heart of God. It was so deep and mysterious that no human eye could see or mind imagine what it was that Jesus was suffering.

As you stand and watch, God's judgement for sin – our sin – is being poured out on Jesus. It's just as the prophet Isaiah foretold when he wrote: 'He was pierced for our transgressions, he was crushed for our iniquities; the punishment that brought us peace was upon him, and by his wounds we are healed'.[25]

Just like a sacrificial lamb – in the darkness – wave after wave of sin pours upon the sinless Saviour, and Jesus becomes the curse of the world. He drowns in our sin on a midnight afternoon.

The darkness showed Jesus was utterly forsaken

Jesus experienced utter abandonment because of our sin. For the very first time in eternity he was separated from the Father. As Jesus cried out, 'My God, My God why have you forsaken me?'[26] the God who could not look upon sin could not look upon his son.

In a way that our human minds will never grasp, the one who had never sinned became sin for us. And God could only turn his face. Father and Son were torn apart. And day became night.

The darkness showed a wound in eternity

In one sense this was an everlasting night. For a God who lives outside of time, those hours on the cross will last forever. Those wounds of Jesus will never heal. His love is from everlasting to everlasting.

And he did it all for us – to make our forgiveness possible.

A way to understand it

What Jesus did for us reminds me of a true story involving two brothers who lived in San Francisco.

The younger brother ran with a street gang. One night during a fight the knife in his hand met the soft flesh of a rival. Death was swift. The young man ran home to exchange blood-stained clothes for clean ones and fled back into the night.

The older brother arrived home soon afterwards – to discover the garments on the floor and police sirens wailing. By the time the police arrived he was wearing the discarded bloody apparel as though it were his own.

Eventually the older brother was charged, tried and

executed for first-degree murder. During all this his younger brother silently witnessed the love of his older sibling – who died in his place and paid his penalty.

Finally it became more than he could bear. Overcome with remorse, he turned himself in and confessed all. But the police sent him away. There could be no charges because his brother's death had fully satisfied the demands of the law. Justice had been done.

And that, in essence, is exactly what God has done for us. To deal with our sin in a way that is both just and loving, he has taken our punishment onto himself. This is what Jesus came to do and is what makes his death so unique.

Three ways to respond

When animals were sacrificed as part of the Jewish religion, there were three ways people responded: the good, the bad, and the ugly.

The 'good' response involved the person taking it seriously. Turning their back on their wrongs, they looked forward to a fresh start with God. They genuinely trusted in God's promise that the blame on their shoulders would be placed on the animal.

A 'bad' response was one of hypocrisy. A sacrifice would be brought only so they could keep on doing wrong. It was sin on easy payments – the more they sinned, the more they brought sacrifices.

The 'ugly' response came from those who couldn't hack the system at all. They just ignored it. They weren't bothered about a relationship with God, and figured they'd worry about their sin when they saw him.

The same is true today. You can choose the way you respond to what Jesus has done for us.

The good way is to believe. The price has been paid. All we have to do is to accept God's forgiveness. Not by just intellectually believing it happened in history but personally claiming Jesus' sacrifice for ourselves.

In this act of faith we actively believe our sin and its consequences have been placed on Jesus – and we are now clean and forgiven.

The bad way is to get religious about it. We can admire the drama, stick rigidly to what Jesus taught, and turn everything into an outward observance – but still fail to make the sacrifice of Jesus personal to us. In this way we are no more than unforgiven admirers.

The ugly way is to reject God's generous offer altogether. How could such a wonderful gift be left neglected and unopened? It's beyond me. It's like getting birthday presents and leaving them wrapped. It means the penalty for our sin remains unpaid – until we ourselves pay its terrible price.

The difference that waits

If you open the gift – if you accept the sacrifice Jesus made as counting for yourself – so much becomes yours.

A clean slate. The payment you owed has been wiped off the books. You are debt free.

And God does something we can't. Ever been told by a friend, 'Forget I told you that'? It's impossible. But God can choose to forget. He puts our sin behind his back and decides never to think of it again.

A clear conscience. There is nothing left for you to feel guilty about. The past is gone. The heavenly delete button has been pressed. The record of your wrong-doings and the penalty due has vanished. There are no back-up copies to haunt you.

A restored relationship. God now sees you as though you had never sinned – because you have been forgiven. So you can now feel clean and comfortable in his presence.

By getting this far you have already made quite a journey. But could there still be some big boulders in the way – in the form of some tough and nagging questions? Just in case, the next two chapters face up to two of the most likely – and the most difficult.

Chapter 9

WAY TO GO

Can God be reached by any road you travel?

You'll have noticed by now that this book is not just about filling your head with new ideas. I'm after your life. You suspected as much? I thought so.

These pages aim to do far more than help you win the right coloured slice of pie next time a question about religion crops up at Trivial Pursuit. It's about information for action. In the end you're going to have to decide whether to jump. This will mean either saying 'thank you but no thanks'. Or actively putting your faith in Jesus, his sacrifice and all that he stands for.

In which case you may wonder if such a decision involves kissing your intellect goodbye. Because there are probably a few heavy-duty questions lurking at the back of your battered mind.

Right now, the idea of taking a step of faith may be as appealing as leaping into a tank filled with alligators, in the hope of finding a promised diamond necklace on the bottom. 'Just have faith!' can sound suspiciously like 'Turn off your brain, hold your nose, and jump!'

Before I do any such thing I need answers. 'Have the alligators been tranquillised? Do they only eat people on alternate Tuesdays?'

It's the same for the issue of faith in God and following Jesus. There are still some big questions out there. And it wouldn't be fair to take you this far and then drop you with a pat on the head and a 'Have a nice life!'

That's why the next two chapters hit full on two of the biggest questions asked when people are weighing up the odds about putting their faith in Jesus and becoming his follower. I'm not saying you will end up with everything nailed down. But let's take an intelligent look. You deserve it.

How can one religion be right out of so many?

Without doubt you know a deeply religious person – or three – who do not focus what they believe on Jesus. Perhaps they are neighbours or friends or your doctor, or run the local curry shop. And, in each case, they are just one of millions around the world who believe what they do.

And you're questioning whether it's reasonable to accept that these nice, sincere, friendly and helpful people can be wrong. Or are they as right as anyone else, because all religions are much the same any way? Does it even matter? And if it does, how can anyone possibly know which to choose out of such a rich assortment?

Come with me on a journey through the supermarket of faith to see if we can find some answers.

Where we can agree

The major faiths on the globe have contributed significantly to our lives and our cultures. For example:

They have added cultural richness. Our planet is a more varied and interesting place to live because of them. Take the beauty of Muslim art and architecture, the haunting strains of

Hindu music, or the liveliness of Jewish feasts and celebrations for example.

These, and so many other traditions, have broadened our appreciation of what it means to be alive, express ourselves and relate to others.

They uphold strong moral values. In many ways the world faiths have been custodians of the values that have kept society from drifting into chaos. These values have been the basis for the principles of law and order which help maintain justice.

They do their best to make sense of the world. All religions point to the fact that human beings are not the centre of the universe. And that there is some reality outside of human life that can make sense of our existence.

They also agree that death is something we must take account of and include in how we view this life.

Are all religions much the same?

Are the major religions of the world much like baked beans? There's a rumour – denied vigorously by Heinz – that there's only one baked bean factory in the known universe. And no matter what brand is on the tin, we all eat the same stuff.

True or not, is that how it is with religions? The label may read Buddhism, Islam, Christianity, Hinduism or whatever – but is the substance inside no different? Do they all worship the same god and have the same nutritional content?

The more you know about baked beans the more convinced you will be that the 'one factory' theory is wide of the mark. The same applies to religion.

Those who know little on the subject may assume only the packaging is different. But it's certainly not a view anyone on the inside of any religion holds. Because they know how starkly different their beliefs are from each other.

What kind of God?

Take the issue of God for example. The major world religions all believe quite different things.

- A Hindu will tell you there are countless gods – who all work to their own set of rules.
- Buddhists don't speak about God or whether he even exists.
- A Muslim will explain that there is only one God but he is unknowable.
- A Christian believes there is only one God and he can be known intimately and personally.

How to keep God on your side

Let's look at it another way. How do the major religions believe you go about staying in God's good books?

- A Muslim will tell you it's by observing a regular system of prayer, fasting and by giving to the poor.
- A Hindu will tell you it's a matter of appeasing the many gods by worshipping at a shrine or an idol, and practising personal discipline.
- A Buddhist believes there is no god to keep in with – but that by looking inward and doing good you will get a better deal next time round.
- A Christian will tell you that the only way to be forgiven is by faith in the sacrifice of Jesus on the cross.

These religions are not even expressing complementary views which go together to form a complete picture. It's not like a diverse group of people describing a new car, with some talking about its performance, others about its engineering and still others about its colour and style.

The views of other faiths are not complementary but actually contradictory. The car's red. No, blue. It's petrol. No, diesel. It's got an eighteen-foot wheel base, six doors, a cocktail cabinet and two fluffy dice on the back shelf. No, it's a two-door mini with Bloggs the Builders emblazoned on the sides.

They are that different. Which leads to a very heavy question.

Do all religions lead to God?

Picture God as a city. Is it true, as some have been heard to say, that all roads lead there? Let's think through this attractive thought.

If God were a city we could approach him by any number of routes. We could take 'Muslim Avenue' or 'Hindu Street'. We could take the 'Christian Boulevard'. Or maybe one of the minor roads we pave ourselves. So many options. Which way should I go to reach my final destination? Perhaps I could do a bit of all of them if I pick the route with care.

But God is not a city – God is a person. If he were a city we could approach him on any given road. And from the air and by tunnels. But, as a person, he is reached only through a relationship – and on his terms.

God has feelings, views, expectations, likes and dislikes – and relates to us on that basis. A city has character, not personality. So while the city limit sign may say 'Welcome' it doesn't have a heart that leaps for joy when you get there.

Isn't sincerity enough?

Even if some religions have got things a bit wrong, isn't it enough to be sincere?

This one's simple. Have you ever been in an argument over something provable? Like how to spell Haagen Dazs. I strongly disagreed with an editor over its spelling earlier in the book. I told him – I *know* how to spell it – H-A-G-E-N – D-A-S!

In the end he went to a shop and bought one – ate it – and then showed me the carton and the correct spelling. What a pig. Not the editor – but the fact I got it wrong.

The point I'm making is, despite my sincerity, the spelling on the carton did not change to accommodate me. In the same way, we all get it sincerely wrong at times. But so far as religion is concerned, does it matter? If you think it doesn't – and remember it's not how to spell some made-up word that we're talking about – let me ask you a question. How come belief in God is the only big issue in the universe for which sincerity is all that matters?

Next time you fly, do you want a pilot who is cast-iron confident about how to land? Or just one who is sincere? Next time you're under the surgeon's knife, do you want him fully up to date with the latest medical training? Or will a good dollop of sincerity be enough? Next time you hit the road for a six-hour journey, do you plan to have a map handy? Or simply set out overdosed on sincerity?

If you are still on the 'sincerity is all that matters' kick, does this mean you admire the sincerity of Stalin, Pol Pot, Idi Amin and such? And that God does too?

You get my drift. Right is right and wrong is wrong, no matter how sincere or insincere we are.

What does Jesus say about other religions?

But never mind my own opinion. Let's turn to someone who has a right to a view – Jesus. What's his verdict on all this? He puts it simply and plainly by saying, 'I am the way, the truth, and the life. No one comes to the Father except through me.'[1]

Pause and read that again. It's worth it. And now let's think through what he is saying, step by step.

Jesus said 'the way.' First he tells us there *is* a road that gets there. The Father – God – *is* reachable.

Jesus said 'the' way, not 'a' way. Second he makes clear that we don't have a variety of possible routes to the end destination. There's not a super highway, a pretty way along the back lanes, and a few others in between. Not a great way, a not-so-good way and a you're-bound-to-get-stuck-behind-caravans way.

It's like the path between two railway stations. There's the rail track or there's the rail track.

Jesus said 'the way' and 'the truth' go together. He makes no mention of sincerity or best guesses. Rather, he links the journey to be made with one of truth.

Please allow me to be technical for a moment. Jesus didn't speak English. And the word he used that has been translated 'truth' is not truth in terms of a fact that is accurate. It's a word that would be used to describe the 'real thing'.

Without doubt you have bought a cheap copy of a designer label garment. What you had was not authentic – and you eventually noticed the difference. It had all the style and swagger of the real thing – on the outside. Then came the test – the first time you washed it. Remember the result? You're probably still using it to clean the car.

Jesus was saying he is the only authentic way to God.

Jesus said 'No one'. By that he meant 'no one'. Or to put it another way, 'no one'. And, if you check out the words he used that we have translated as 'no one', you will find they mean – wait for it – 'no one'.

By now you have probably got the picture.

What makes Jesus so different?

What lies at the heart of Jesus' astonishing claim is the stark contrast between him and every other religious leader or founder of a religion. Jesus is uniquely the way because he alone deals with the three greatest issues of life.

He pays our debt

All the other religions of the world demand their followers do something in order to work their way to God. They may each propose different things but the message is the same – do enough and get it right and you'll be OK . . . maybe.

It's the religious version of the reward cards you get in supermarkets. The ones where you spend £3,000 with the shop and they give you enough 'reward vouchers' to buy a six-pack and a bag of nappies. That's what earning points is like the world over. And that's what the religions of the world expect you to do. Some people even wrongly think this is the way Christianity works. That it's all down to earning points with God – redeemable vouchers for the end of time.

In their mind they will one day stand in line at the gates of heaven where a celestial checkout girl says, 'OK, so let's weigh up all the bad things you've done. Hmmmm. And can I see your vouchers, please? That's quite a stack there – let me count 'em up. Oh dear. What a shame you didn't peg it when you had that heart attack a few years back. You were in credit then. Now you're four vouchers short.'

God isn't like that. He doesn't enslave us to the eternal 'weights and balances', so that we're for ever trying to make up for the wrong things we have done. And never knowing whether or not we've done enough.

While this is the treadmill other religions put people on, Jesus offers something completely different. When it comes to the eternal checkout counter the welcome that's available is 'I see your debts have been paid by Jesus' death on the cross. And since you've trusted in him, come on in.'

While all other religions ask followers to earn points to claim the prize that can never be earned – Jesus gives the gift away freely to any who will accept it. His death on the cross paid for all the wrong things any of us have done – as long as we accept his payment.

He gives us the strength we need

While other religions tell us how to live, Jesus gives us the power to live. The full details come in a later chapter but let me just touch on the principles.

The problem with religion is, it can never change a person's heart. But Jesus can. What he offers is not only forgiveness and a new start but a new operating system. Or, to put it in terms of what a decayed house needs – a complete re-wiring.

That's not a perfect illustration. But it gets to the heart of the issue. When we put our faith in all that Jesus did – and commit our lives to him – God does the same for us as he did for Jesus. He raises us from the dead – spiritually. We actually become 'alive to God' in a way we never were before.

He provides a dynamic relationship

The other thing Jesus offers that no religion does, is a living relationship with God himself. I can't be friends with a law or a creed or a dogma. But only with a person.

We are not left to treat God like a set of rules to be broken and then pieced back together again. God is not law – he is alive. He's a living person – someone who longs to know us.

Is it any wonder Jesus is the only way, when he alone offers:

- the certainty of forgiveness – through his death on the cross
- a new spiritual life – through his power in us
- a new relationship – through his personal companionship.

What a way to go!

What happens to those who sincerely get it wrong

If all the above is true we still have to face a very awkward question. Would a loving God really thumb his nose at good people who climbed the wrong tree in their sincere search to find him? Would he really lock them out of his presence because they never heard or understood the good news about Jesus?

My honest answer is, I don't know how God will deal with those jungle tribesmen from the back of beyond or my Muslim friends who run the local corner shop. Or what his plans are for my accountant who follows an ancient religion from the East. And I don't need to know. Issues like that are best left to God himself.

What I do know is, whatever happens, God will be absolutely fair about it. And such is his character, he would be more likely to look for excuses to get people into heaven than for reasons to keep them out.

But I also know, if there were some other way for sin to be forgiven other than through the sacrifice of his son, God would have taken it.

I do know that, however it ends up, these people I so love and respect are missing out on the exhilarating joy of going through life with a clear conscience and the companionship of the God who made them.

Finally, having faced a barrage of your questions, allow me one of my own. If there is a way to reach God, have you taken it?

Now, with one big road block to belief out of the way, here comes another – and it's the question more often asked than any other.

Chapter 10

WHAT A PAIN

Isn't there just too much suffering to believe?

If you could ask God one question what would it be? 'What numbers will be on the lottery balls next Saturday?' Or 'Why did you make wasps?'

That's not the response most people would give. I know because a UK national newspaper paid a research company big money to find out what was the number one question their readers would like to ask the Almighty. And at number one, for the three hundredth week running, it was: 'If you are so good and powerful, why don't you stop all the suffering?'

It's a fair question, even if we can't answer it completely. But let's give it our best shot.

The world is in pain

No one in their right mind would disagree that life hurts. Horrendous images flash across our TV screens daily, until our minds are almost numb with the horror of it all. The bloodbath of genocide in Rwanda, the devastation of war in Bosnia, life-destroying drought in the Sudan, hurricanes in Central America, floods in Bangladesh.

Stark pictures cling to our minds – of weeping children,

distraught mothers and battle-scarred victims. And that's just what happens 'out there'.

Closer to home, we've lived through Lockerbie, Dunblane, murders of children by children, senseless killings in Northern Ireland and terrorist bombs which decimate entire city districts, carrying the innocent in their wake.

I'm not doing so great either

We can 'solve' most of the suffering 'out there' with the flick of a TV remote control. War, famine and the rest can give way to the cosy cheerfulness of an episode of *Friends* in a twinkling. That's not true of the pain closer to home.

The devastating blast comes when we or those we love are struck down. Perhaps you've cried with a friend betrayed by their partner or exploded over the life-stunting effects of sexual abuse committed within a family. AIDS, cancer, depression, redundancy and a host of other evils can storm through our lives, leaving us wounded and gasping.

Even just scanning the names in my address list brings an ache. There are the friends whose first child died within days of its birth. Another whose wife has almost wasted away from multiple sclerosis. Another whose wife died in a car accident. Another who suffered the betrayal of her husband's ten-year secret affair. Another whose cherished first child will never walk. Another whose mother suffered from Alzheimer's.

What unites them all is pain and the reasonable question, 'If God is so wonderful, why does life hurt so much?'

As for me, I don't have a corner on the personal pain market but I've shopped there. My father died a lingering death from lung cancer when I was 17. The big 'C' struck again when my wife Rosemary developed thyroid cancer at thirty. Physically she came through, but depression plagued her for the following four years.

And my own voice joined the chorus 'Why?'

Where do we start to answer the question of suffering?

How do we reconcile a world of pain, suffering and injustice with a God who seems not to care a fig or lift a finger?

We need to start with God, as he's the one in the dock. Let's first remind ourselves of what he is like. And let me explain why.

My colleague Donna Vann remembers the time her daughter came bouncing home from infant school with a 'stitchery' picture she'd lovingly sewn. It had started out as a piece of paper printed with the design of a flower. Little Lisa had attempted to sew coloured thread around the outlines and managed to prick herself in the process.

The finished work of art – so proudly presented – was crumpled and stained with the evidence of her endeavour. And the stitching looked more like a clump of weeds than a flower. The only way to make sense of this masterpiece was to take a fresh look at the original background.

In the same way any investigation of the unknown needs to begin from the point of what is known.

So is God a cosmic sadist who rejoices over inflicting pain on creatures who can't fight back? Or is he a bumbling, ineffectual designer? Is this world, as Van Gogh put it, 'one of his sketches that turned out badly'?

Actually, the opposite is true. The backdrop of the Big Picture is that God has demonstrated his love for us with the most overwhelming of proof. He loves us enough to cause himself pain on our behalf — because that's what happened when he sent Jesus. Far from enjoying the spectacle of us suffering, he entered our world and suffered with us. And any attempt to make sense of pain and suffering has to begin by locking on to the unchanging co-ordinates of God's love.

So, as a starting point, let's assume God does care terribly about us – even if you don't feel it – and see where it might lead us.

Clues to the problem of suffering?

First, here's a piece of outstanding honesty. If there were one clear and simple answer to why God lets people suffer, you could bottle it and make a fortune. It is an even greater mystery than which way up a cat would fall if you strapped a piece of buttered toast to its back and dropped it.

There is no one easy done-and-dusted answer waiting in the wings. Instead it's a bit like putting together a jigsaw puzzle – hopefully not as bad as the 1000-piece picture of writhing earthworms.

Let's take it one chunk at a time. Corner pieces first.

It's mostly our fault

Who really is to blame for the catalogue of pain and ills that stomp down on us daily? A newspaper report I saw recently reinforces the question. 'The boat did it, honest!' was the headline. A 70-foot yacht started up, broke loose and went on a spree across a harbour in Florida, smashing other vessels and a marina to the tune of seven million dollars in damage. Whose fault was it? Thieves, vandals, a careless sailor?

Not at all. Investigators are convinced the yacht, appropriately named Hat Trick, got up to the prank all by itself.

Want to bet the owner felt like blaming God? That's what we do. As if God left the bow doors open on the Zeebrugge ferry, or personally spilt the 72,000 tonnes of crude oil from the *Sea Empress*. As if God personally planted all the landmines now randomly blowing legs off innocent children. As if God was responsible for the inefficient management of the Union Carbide factory in Bhopal, India, where lethal gas leaks killed 2,000 and poisoned 200,000 more. Or caused the meltdown at the Chernobyl nuclear power station that wreaked havoc across Northern Europe.

It's as if God is responsible for vandals who de-rail trains and thieves who prey on pensioners, drunken drivers who commit motorway murder, governments who let their people starve while the leaders live in luxury.

Much of what causes us pain in this life is the result of human selfishness or greed. It is people, not God, who have produced racks, whips, knives, guns, bayonets and bombs. And it is not God who makes sure the world powers spend some £10,000 million on military arms every two weeks – enough to give all the world adequate food, water, education and health for a year.

Much of the suffering of the innocent is directly down to us. Maybe not us personally, but at least we can't write it off to God.

Like Miss Piggy's perfume, we proudly wear a label that says 'Moi' and behave that way – with painful consequences. We cause others to suffer by unkind actions, thoughtless words, or even just by 'I can't be bothered' to help someone in need.

Even many natural disasters can be traced back to us. Human greed, thoughtlessness and cynical exploitation has damaged the environment – and lies at the root of many of these so-called 'natural' disasters.

The message? If we point our finger at God there are three pointing back at us.

God allows us the dignity of human choice

God could stop all this foolishness. Surely he would if he cared! After all, if you see a child with a sharp object you take it away. If they are heading down the street you hold their hand. If a truck is about to mow them down you snatch them to safety. Why doesn't God do the same?

He could if you wanted to be a child all your life – never free to make your own decisions, never having the dignity of growing to maturity. But that wouldn't be a life – that would be a nursery.

God could programme people so they never make mistakes or behave badly. But do you want to live on a whole planet full of android types like Kryten from Red Dwarf? What bliss! What perfection! 'I'm sorry sir, I just can't help being good and serving others all the time. It's all I'm programmed to do!' We would have no wars nor even two people having a disagreement. But they would not be human. And, as you would be one of them, neither would you.

God is powerful enough to remove all evil from the earth, if that's the way he wanted to play it. But would you want it? Do you fancy living in a place like Seahaven, the TV-location-city featured in the Jim Carrey film *The Truman Show*? This controlled environment was populated by people pushing baby carriages, riding bicycles, and cleaning their spotless houses in exactly the same way every day for all of time. And all presided over by the watchful benevolent producer – God.

For everyone in Seahaven, except Truman, this was adequate – because they were actors. But Truman wasn't scripted by the cosmic producer. He was a real, living human with needs and desires and frustrations, which eventually made him yearn to break out of the perfect world.

We can't have it both ways. Either we will be in Seahaven as robots living according to script, or on a planet where we are allowed the dignity of choice. And once we get to choose, sometimes we will choose harm – to ourselves and to others.

God could eradicate anyone who may cause suffering to another. But how long before he'd come knocking on my door – or yours? He might start with the big baddies like terrorists and tyrants, but eventually he would show up where I live. And you could be next.

We live in a spoiled world

We can just about get our heads around human selfishness as a cause of innocent suffering, but how about situations where no human is involved? Like, for example, birth defects. Disease which takes the life of a child. Or Alzheimer's.

This question takes us back to the way it all began. Because something happened early on in the history of the world which has affected us ever since.

People were given a choice to live by the Maker's guidelines, and they decided not to. They ignored his instructions, and he let them. He did not force them to obey. But their stubborn refusal to listen had tragic consequences.

What happened then reminds me of the night of 14 April, 1912 when the *Titanic* was warned six times by radio from the ship *Californian* of icebergs in its path. But the self-sufficient we'll-do-it-our-way *Titanic* crew turned a deaf ear. Crewman John Phillips finally told the *Californian* to 'shut up'.

That night 1522 people died needlessly. The disaster could have been avoided, if only the instructions had been heeded.

Remember the word 'sin'? Each of us has the equivalent of our own Millennium Bug – a malfunction that veers us toward selfishness and doing it our way. If this were limited to temper tantrums it wouldn't be so bad. But when it rears its ugly head in relationships, in the way we drive, the way we manage the economy, the way we treat other nations, it's a whole different bag.

All of creation slipped off balance when rebellion came into the world. 'I'll do it my way, God. Shut up and mind your own business.' Sickness and pain were not in the original script but were added later by humanity. It could have been otherwise, but we had the choice.

Our understanding is limited

Suppose there are answers to the huge questions but they are beyond our ability to grasp? Even if God did sit down with us over a cup of coffee to explain the whole reason for suffering in the world, would he have to use vocabulary we never learned and mathematical terms we couldn't comprehend?

Compared to God, we're like children who assume – often wrongly – that we're big enough to understand everything. In my book *Pressure Points* I tell a personal story that's worth repeating because it illustrates perfectly what I mean.

Of all the traumas to have befallen our children, the one that haunts me the most concerns our third son, Aran, when he was about five years old. Running across our back garden at his frenetic speed, he tripped. Head and garden bench collided, badly tearing the corner of Aran's eyelid. One glance confirmed it was a stitches job and we made our familiar route to the hospital.

The necessary stitches required a local anaesthetic, but the injection did not allow him to look the other way. The result was an agonising ten minutes while I physically held Aran down in order for the essential treatment to take place. There, wrapped in my arms and doggedly fighting, his very best interests were being served. From his fearful and confused perspective, I was contributing to his pain. All he could say was 'Daddy' as we both cried together.

Like Aran, if only we could see things from a perspective other than our own, then perhaps we would understand a little more.

God responds to our pain

Is pain all bad? Not necessarily. Some of the most beautiful people I know are those who have suffered. And this is particularly true of those who have worked out their suffering in the context of their faith in God.

Indeed, God may seem closer and more real in times of pain. The author CS Lewis, who lost his wife to cancer early on in their marriage, observed, 'God whispers to us in our pleasures, speaks in our conscience, but shouts in our pain.'

That may not be the reason for our pain but many – including myself – would be poorer people without it.

An outstanding example is my friend Joni Eareckson Tada. As an attractive teenager she enjoyed riding horses and an effervescent social life. One warm July day, while swimming with her sister, she dived into the lake that was far too shallow for her safety. She had left the diving board as a carefree teenager – and was pulled out of the water as a quadriplegic.

Joni went through agonies of doubt, anger with God, and bitterness at being imprisoned in a body that didn't work. Finally, she allowed her situation to draw her closer to God. Today she travels throughout the world as a champion for the disabled. 'I wouldn't change my life for anything,' she says. 'I even feel privileged.'

The last time I was with her she told me, 'What's all the fuss? Compared with eternity, this life and its suffering will be over in an instant. Then I will have a perfect body for ever. And I'll dance!'

God not only uses our pain to make himself more real, he shares our pain with us. For a start, he's been there. He knows what it feels like. In Jesus, he experienced every emotion known that we can know – except a feeling of guilt, because he never did wrong. As God the Father, he had to watch his precious son die a cruel death. And every minute of every day he feels the pain of rejection from people who just don't want to know.

Let me take you back again to my son Aran and his eye. As I held him I not only saw suffering in a clearer perspective but also how God must feel. In the same way that I held my son I realised God wants us to be fully engulfed in his loving embrace. He is not interested in sympathising from a distance, but longs to be personally and intimately involved in our experience.

If we could see pain and suffering from God's perspective perhaps we would even discover that we aren't the only ones crying. His eyes are also wet with tears.

A mystery still remains

Still, when all is said and done, there is no complete and satisfying reply to the pain-driven question, 'Why?' But it is not a question you absolutely must solve before responding to God's offer of forgiveness and a new life. It may even be a reason for making such a step – because the more you discover about God and his love the more likely you are to understand.

At the same time God doesn't rap us on the knuckles for asking the question. Let the following story soak into your heart. It's a story that's been in circulation for some while, though where it came from no one seems to know. It brings a totally different perspective to the issue of suffering.

The Long Silence

At the end of time, billions of people were scattered on a great plain before God's throne. Most shrank back from the brilliant light before them. But some groups near the front talked heatedly, not with cringing shame but with belligerence.

'Can God judge us? What does he know about suffering?' snapped a woman with dark hair. Her body showed the telltale ravages of the torture chamber. 'I've endured terror . . . beating . . . rape . . . death!'

In another group, a young African opened his shirt. 'What about this?' he demanded, revealing the bullet holes. 'Killed for no crime but belonging to the wrong tribe!'

In another crowd, a young man with sullen eyes: 'I've got AIDS,' he murmured. 'Why me? Why should I suffer?'

Far out across the plain were hundreds of such groups. Each had a complaint against God for the evil and suffering he had permitted in his world. How lucky God was to live in heaven where everything was sweetness and light, where there was no weeping or fear, no hunger or hatred. What did God know of all that the human race had been forced to endure? For God leads a pretty sheltered life, they said.

So each of these groups sent out a leader, chosen because he or she had suffered most – someone who had been killed by a bomb, a murder victim, a horribly deformed arthritic, someone born with brain damage, an abused child . . . In the centre of the plain these leaders consulted with each other. At last they were ready to present their case. It was rather clever.

Before God could be qualified to be their judge, he must endure what they endured. They decided that God should be sentenced to live on earth – as a man!

Let him be born a Jew. Let people think him illegitimate. Let him live in a country occupied and ruled by a cruel, callous government. Give him a work so difficult that even his family would think him out of his mind when he tried to do it. Let him be betrayed by his closest friends.

Let him face false charges, be tried by a prejudiced jury and convicted by a cowardly judge. Let him be beaten and tortured. At the last, let him see what it means to be terribly alone. Then let him die. Let him die so that there can be no doubt that he died. Let there be a host of witnesses to his death.

As each leader announced his or her portion of the sentence, loud murmurs of approval went up from the throng of people assembled. When the last person had finished pronouncing sentence, there was a long silence. No one uttered a word. No one moved. For suddenly all knew that God had already served his sentence.[1]

Chapter 11

JUST DESSERTS

What about pie in the sky when we die?

According to the very latest statistics, the current death rate stands at 100 per cent. Feel free to look at the small print of your 'Right to be a Human on the Planet Earth' contract – but you'll find the 'Life Termination' section has no get-out clause.

Everyone on the globe will one day breath their last. When I go I want to die peacefully in my sleep – like my grandfather did. Not screaming like the passengers in his car.

And how can anyone write about death without including the famous Woody Allen quote? He said, 'I'm not afraid to die. It's just that I don't want to be there when it happens.'

But we *will* be there – and what then?

What happens when we die?

Beliefs on the 'after death what' front seem to fall into three basic categories.

The big snuff. Some believe death is simply El Finito – the end. That at the moment the body quits breathing and the brain stops flickering you are as dead as mutton. It's goodbye and goodnight – with no wake-up call – ever.

They sincerely believe the best you can hope for is that life will be nice while it lasts. But this is all you're going to get.

Despite our present high-tech rational world, the belief that this life is all there is, doesn't seem to be gathering momentum. For all the money and energy being spent on prolonging life down here in a desperate attempt to keep the inevitable at bay, there seems to be no lack of people who believe there's more to life than this.

One more time. Cosmic recycling is at the heart of this belief. Far from being the end, this life is just one stepping stone in an ongoing metamorphosis. Depending on how well you did last time you'll come back as someone – or something – else.

Belief in reincarnation has been around for a long time. The ancient Greek philosopher Plato, for example, wrote 'A bad man's fate is to be reincarnated as a woman.' There will be plenty of women who hope that Plato's fate was somewhat worse than that.

The concept is that our soul will live a succession of lives. In each we are born, live and die – and then come back to do it all over again. As a cockroach or a king. Or something in between. It's an idea that appeals to our innate desire to get it right. You can mess up in this life but still have another chance.

Heaven here I come. This is a belief that there's an existence we can consciously experience after death. Different cultures call it different things – Heaven, Nirvana, Elysium, the Happy Hunting Ground and so on.

Through the centuries people have been buried with their belongings in the belief they will be needing them in their next destination. The Egyptian rulers did it in style. In other cultures the dead man's wife was thrown on the funeral pyre with him – added to his baggage allowance in the assumption he would be needing her in the future.

How can we know?

Some argue we can't know anything about a possible after-life until we get there – or don't as the case may be. But could there be some clues?

Our mind tells us. Apart from the emotional tugs of wishing to believe that this life isn't all there is, there is also a logic to it. Can you imagine trying to convince an unborn baby that life in the womb was all there was going to be? But why have I got arms? Why have I got legs? What am I supposed to do with them? There must be something more?

What are we meant to do with the knowledge we are assimilating, the character we are building and the spiritual dimension we are developing? Is it really to be put to no good use? Is the womb of this world all there is?

We intuitively sense it. There seems to be so much more than wishful thinking when it comes to believing that beyond all this is something greater and 'different'.

Throughout the ages there has been a deep-seated belief – a kind of 'given' – that there is another reality outside and beyond us of which we are part from the moment of death.

Experience supports it. A well-documented phenomenon is the near-death experience – NDE – which no self-respecting cardiac arrest victim seems able to avoid these days. You have heard stories of someone 'dying' on the operating slab to find themselves wafting along a long dark tunnel towards a bright light, before being ushered into a world of great beauty. Then a voice tells them, 'It's not your time to die – you have to go back.' Occasionally the voice adds, 'And save the world.'

Until recently NDE's were all nice warm fuzzy ones. But others are now surfacing. A recent report spoke of it becoming clear that for some people, NDE's are far from blissful. Instead of a feeling of floating upwards, they report being pulled downwards – towards a pit inhabited by demons. The article commented on 'the eerie parallels between the reports of NDE's and traditional views of heaven and hell.'[1]

It's possible for such experiences to be down to the medication they are receiving or brain activity under extreme stress. And hard evidence one way or the other is impossible.

What did Jesus say about life after death?

The best credentials for speaking about life after death belong to Jesus. After all, human theories and debatable experiences don't hold a match to his first-hand knowledge of death and his authority as God.

Based on the things Jesus told us on earth, we can be sure of the following:

It's a place where Jesus is. To the man being crucified with him, Jesus said, 'I promise that today you will be with me in paradise.' So 'paradise', which gets to be called 'heaven' elsewhere, exists and Jesus is there.[2]

It's for ever. The picture Jesus used to explain heaven to his followers was of a spacious mansion with many rooms. 'I'm going to get things ready for you,' he told them.[3]

One of the UK's most watched TV programmes involves different families each decorating a room of the other's house. And they go to infinite trouble to do the very best for one another. In heaven – Jesus is taking the trouble to make everything perfect for those who follow him. Does that blow your mind? It should.

The reason behind his work, promised Jesus, was so that he and his followers would always be together.[4] That means there is no check-out time, passing Go to collect £200, or a further hop round the board again. Heaven, says Jesus, is a permanent and on-going experience.

It's a great place to be. Heaven, says Jesus, is the ideal place to store what you treasure – because there are no thieves, no moths and no decay.[5] What could be better – no sin, no bugs and nothing ever needs mending. These three are at the top of my must-avoid list of items. Particularly if spiders are included in the moth category.

It's a place for those who have pre-registered. Jesus said that heaven's a place where the names of its intended residents are written down.[6] Those who look to be in heaven need to have their names on the list before they get there.

These earthly pictures of a heavenly environment help us to wrap our minds round the unknown as best as we are able. But there will always be a limit to what we can grasp because the building fabric of eternity is unlike anything we have ever seen or experienced.

I remember sitting under a tree in a third world village where electricity had yet to arrive. I was trying – and failing – to explain to a family the principles of a washing machine and tumble drier. For us, grasping the realities of the world beyond is even harder.

It also reminds me of a small girl from the city who was visiting her grandmother in the country. While taking a walk one evening the girl was overwhelmed at the brilliance of the stars.

'Gran,' she exclaimed, 'if heaven is so pretty on the wrong side, imagine what it must be like on the right side!'

Pretty or not, let's face it, don't you honestly have a secret fear that to anyone other than the Pope, heaven will be as exciting as listening to worms singing? And we will have to do it for ever.

The problem is that heaven has been poorly served by its public relations office. The big travel companies have invested millions to sell the sizzle of faraway places from Mali to Madagascar. But all heaven has had to fight back with have been a few cartoons showing old people on clouds.

And isn't it hard to get your mind round the idea of doing anything – however wonderful – for longer than two or three weeks at a stretch?

But do we really believe the eternal God who created creativity has no more in mind for us than everlasting boredom? As God is there, heaven must surely be the most exhilarating, mind-blowing, ever-changing, always something-up-his-sleeve place. We may not be able to picture it but if the limited environment of Earth keeps throwing up surprises, the potential of heaven is unimaginable.

Heaven was not the only place Jesus spoke about

Please don't overlook exactly who Jesus was speaking to when he said all this about heaven. It wasn't to all and sundry. In every case the message was to people who were following him.

Miss that point and you could assume that Jesus wanted us to believe heaven was the place where everyone goes. But that isn't the full picture. Jesus spoke about two separate destinations and a point after death where some people went one way and some the other.

Two destinations

Jesus explained that after death followed judgement – and he was to be the judge. To help them picture what he meant, the great teacher used two examples that his listeners would be really familiar with:

Jesus said it is like dividing sheep from goats. This happened each evening. After a day together in the fields the two kinds of animal went different ways for the night. It was the shepherd's job to divide them up – which was not always easy as Mediterranean sheep and goats look almost the same as each other. The unruly goats went one way, and the placid sheep the other.[7]

Jesus said it is like separating wheat from chaff. This was an annual event. Every harvest time, as the result of some beating and fanning, the worthless chaff ended up in a different place from the valuable wheat. One went to make food for the hungry. The other went to be burned.[8]

Jesus used these familiar pictures to express as simply and plainly as possible the truth that everyone will face judgement following their death. Sheep and goats all got along fine for long hours on end, and the wheat grew up in the field unimpaired by its unproductive element – chaff. But the day of division and destiny would come.

Our future depends on the issue of forgiveness

Jesus spoke of judgement as being based not on what the animals and the wheat had done – but because of what they were. He didn't speak of good animals divided from bad animals or rebellious wheat set apart from compliant wheat. It was their very nature that decided their different destinations.

This is because it is essentially what we are that will impact us in eternity. The judgement we will face depends on whether we are forgiven or unforgiven.

God doesn't weigh up our good deeds or bad deeds – like cabbages in a market. He looks to see what clothes we are wearing. Is it our old unforgiven, sin-stained, not-in-here-thank-you outfit we have insisted hanging onto? Or the snow-drift white, bleach-clean, glow-in-the-dark new outfit that came as a gift from Jesus along with his forgiveness?

And those who are forgiven will go to be with God forever. While those who haven't, won't.

To be in God's presence, transformed – changed like Cinderella – wearing the new frock of forgiveness, will be a great place to be. Such joy, such an intense sense of belonging and of being where we were always intended to be. But for those who stand before him like an ugly sister, with only their sin to cover them, it will be a soul-searing experience.

Don't blame God

It's not God's fault our sin makes us unwelcome in his presence. It's the result of our choice. Forgiveness was available – through faith in Jesus' death on the cross. But it went unclaimed.

'Take your umbrella,' warned my wife. It was good advice. 'I'll be fine,' came my reply. And I returned home soaked to the skin. But don't blame the rain. I had a choice.

Eternity is where all that you decided on earth comes to its fulfilment. If knowing God personally was not an attractive option down here, why should it be any more attractive for eternity?

In the same way, in eternity, God's breath of love will be a fragrant cooling breeze to one person but to another it will be like a burning scorching flame.

The light of God's presence will either be sunshine to bathe in – or a million-watt bulb that makes us desperate for cover, like cockroaches blinded by the light.

If your whole life – in all your choices – you have opted for 'not God', why at the end of it would you suddenly want to choose him?

You will have had all your life to make it clear to God what you want. Why should he disappoint you now? And it would be immoral of him to force on you something you never wanted.

Imagine a great party in full swing – with everyone dressed up to the tens. It's that kind of do. Laughter shakes the walls. The dress code is all posh frocks and the coolest suits. Everyone knows everyone and they are enjoying each other's company. What a great place to be. But there in the middle, in full gaze of everyone is you – butt naked and alone. Not knowing anyone and with nothing to contribute. You don't even speak their language. And you are there for ever.

Is that where you want to be? No way. You are in the wrong place. And it hurts.

Today's choices matter for ever

Some years ago Donna Vann learned she had cancer. As a result, she endured the emotional pain of possibly having to leave her family behind. And the thought of a lingering, painful death filled her with dread.

But what didn't fill her head was worry about what would happen to her after she died. 'I knew that was settled,' she says. 'Having put my trust in Jesus Christ for forgiveness some years earlier, I was sure my future would be with him.'

Donna's choice had settled it. She had chosen life.

Jesus spoke about the need to choose between two roads. One of which leads to eternal life and the other to destruction.[9] These are his words, not mine.

He could well have been standing at such a junction when he said it. From the fork in the road two paths stretched into the distance and out of sight. Both had different destinations.

Our greatest choice in life is to accept the road to forgiveness – so that we can stand before him without shame.

There's no sitting on the fence

When you come to a place where the road divides you have to make a choice.

I remember being given tickets to watch my football team playing in an important league match. Unfortunately the seats were right in the middle of the other team's highly vocal supporters. I have never felt so uncomfortable or so vulnerable. When our side scored it was bad enough – having to contain my joy. But when the other side scored it was even worse – having to pretend I was pleased.

It reminds me that in terms of our relationship with God there is no such thing as neutrality. We are either for him or against him. Forgiven because of Jesus – or not. On the broad road or the narrow one.

Can we count on Jesus to lead us home?

Jesus said of himself, 'Those who believe in me will have eternal life'.[10]

When you were a child, can you remember a time when you were dragged off to some event where everyone else was a grown-up? All you could do was hang on to the big safe hand and wait for the time to go home. You couldn't get there yourself – or you would have. But you knew that sometime soon the person you were trusting would take you there safely.

That's how I feel about Jesus. When the time comes to step through the doorway of death, because I have received his forgiveness, I believe he can be trusted to get me home.

Chapter 12

BELIEVE IT OR NOT

Faith, foolishness or futility?

Faith is a confusing business. We're told it can move mountains. But most people opt for dynamite and bulldozers. The cry goes up 'keep the faith' – but what kind of container do they have in mind?

And there's all the stuff about blind faith and a leap of faith. Both of which can sometimes be responsible for some very strange behaviour.

Take, for example, the motorist who tried to explain his car crash to a Munich court by saying he took his hands off the wheel because 'I wanted to know, so I let go and asked: "God, can you drive?"'

That bozo was only marginally dumber than the man who set the cruise control on his huge motor home – and went into the back to make a sandwich. Which is also a true story.

What faith isn't

Words like 'faith' and 'belief' are at the very heart of all we're talking about, so it's essential to be clear as to what they mean.

Faith is not in your genes

The ability to 'believe' or to 'have faith' is not something you inherit – like being able to sing in tune, wriggle your ears or learn a foreign language with ease.

Faith is not a talent, dolloped out generously to some who then become 'religious' – while others are forever destined to be doubters and free of any responsibility. Faith is an ability within all of us – like breathing.

After all, a loving God would never ask us to do something that is beyond our ability to achieve. To insist we believe when having no capacity to do so would be like throwing a stick for a legless dog and shouting 'fetch'.

Faith is not foolishness

Nor is genuine faith blind or irrational – abandoning ourselves to something that makes no sense at all. It isn't as one little boy sweetly said, 'Believing in something you know isn't true.'

The faith we are talking about is not like a placebo happy pill – that does you good even though there is no substance to it. Or just a nice fantasy that makes you feel better – like the idea that if I ever had a one-to-one with Michelle Pfeiffer she'd think I was rather wonderful.

Nor is real faith something that lacks a realistic foundation – as when an image of the face of Christ 'miraculously appeared' on a wall in a Central American city and soon became a shrine with flowers and candles. The image turned out to be a poster for a Willie Nelson concert that someone had whitewashed over.

Three kinds of faith

The words 'faith' and 'belief' are used in so many different ways it's easy to get confused. Let me try to untangle the knots.

Automatic faith

There is a run-of-the-mill kind of faith we use a hundred times a day without thinking. It happens automatically – like blinking.

We have faith that the letter we posted will get there, faith our credit card will work, faith that what is pictured on the packet is actually inside. We may be let down some of the time, but this 'automatic' faith basically keeps us going.

Sustaining faith

There is also a dimension to faith which involves us in trusting in someone or something to come up with the goods on a regular basis. It may be faith in a rabbit's foot and the stars, or that everything works out in the end, or that good always wins, or in a God who cares.

This is a moment-by-moment 'sustaining' faith which impacts our actions and attitudes day by day.

Saving faith

This is an act of faith that transforms our situation. It's the moment when you leap into the arms of the fire fighter as the building burns. It's the decision to put yourself unreservedly into the hands of the surgeon. It's the commitment to trust yourself to the guide when you are lost and a long way from home.

And this is the type of once-and-for-all faith Jesus spoke of when he said, 'Whoever believes in the Son has eternal life; but whoever rejects the Son will not see life for God's wrath remains on him'.[1] Jesus asks us to take what we believe about him and to express it as faith in him – which is saving faith. In other words, what we believe with our mind is acted on by our will in order to make a difference to the way things turn out.

Let's put it this way. You have just fallen into a large vat of slowly acting acid which will gradually eat into your body and destroy you. I don't know how it happened. Didn't your mother warn you about getting into a mess like this?

But here you are and your destruction is certain – unless you make a choice. And here comes the opportunity. To your door comes the Acid Antidote man – he also sells brushes and cuddly toys. 'I've got the very thing you need,' he promises. 'Stand on one leg and take a good swig of this.'

'I don't like the colour,' you reply. 'And maybe it won't work. And I'd feel such a fool.'

'It really will work,' he insists. 'It's been working for two thousand years. And it's worked for me.'

'Let me think about it,' are your last words – and they may well be.

The help you needed was at hand but you refused to believe. The 'wrath' of the acid is still active. You are in big trouble. Your future could have been very different had you acted with saving faith.

It is what our faith is in that matters

The biggest issue of all is not the size of our faith but who or what our faith is in. For example, there you are about to leap from an aeroplane to make a sponsored parachute jump. You did the training, understand the techniques, and believe the physics of billowing parachutes will not let you down – other than gently.

For your first jump you were free to choose your own

parachute – from three options. One had blood stains on the outside and a tag saying 'Second-hand – one unlucky owner'. The next had a note saying 'Packed by the Scouts to raise funds'. The third was in the hands of your instructor – he packed it himself and had double-checked everything.

Which one are you wearing? I thought so. Because it is what our faith is in that matters. In fact, that's all that matters. A small faith in the right parachute is never worth trading for an overwhelming faith in the wrong one. Take my word for it. Please.

In the same way, when I want to reheat a plate of meat and two veg, the microwave is where my faith is. I believe it can do it and I trust it to do so. The same slice of faith placed in our elegant new fridge will leave me cold.

When it comes to having our sinfulness forgiven and receiving the gift of everlasting life, Jesus is where our faith – however small – has to be placed. The same amount of faith in anything or anyone else will leave us unforgiven by God and without the eternal life he promised.

Faith involves action

Some years ago the Hoover Electrical Appliance company foolishly offered two free international flights to anyone spending at least £100 on an appliance. Unbelievable? But it was true – and Rosemary and I believed it.

Most of the people we knew believed too. But their belief didn't extend to action. For whatever reason, they couldn't be bothered to go through the rigmarole involved in sending off receipts and confirming availability of flights. But we did.

Hoover said it. We believed it. Oh how we believed it. And we ended up with two free flights to Florida – all for the price of a vacuum cleaner we needed anyway. Meanwhile we lost count of the number of friends who said, 'Well you would!'

But they could have – had they believed. I mean really believed.

It's like someone whose hands and face are caked with dirt and grime saying with a confident smile, 'I believe in soap.' Ask what they mean and they say, 'Well, I believe soap is a good thing and to be much admired. I believe soap has made a great difference in world history. I believe soap has a lot to offer. I believe soap would get me clean if I were to use it.'

In the same way, so far as Jesus is concerned, he does not ask us merely to admire the excellence of his life or the quality of his words – but to place our saving faith in his sacrifice for us and so receive the benefit.

Simple steps to saving faith

There's a story Jesus told that helps to explain what faith that saves means. It centres on a son who left the family home with the advance payment of his inheritance, blew the lot and ended up eating pig-food.

Eventually the young man came to his senses and hit the road for home – planning to beg forgiveness and ask for a job as a servant in his father's home. Instead, the father – who had been watching and waiting – ran to embrace him, welcomed him back as his son and threw a humdinger of a party in his honour.[2]

Jesus told the story to explain the sheer joy in God's heart when those who have strayed from him come home. But it also conveys how saving faith works. Follow it through with me – because these are the steps each of us must take if we are to receive and experience God's forgiveness.

A realisation of need. There among the pigs and the swill the young man faced up to reality. He was in a mess and totally unable to do anything about it through his own efforts. This is where our own journey towards saving faith has to begin – with our eyes wide open to the mess we're in.

A decision to seek forgiveness. Next he needed to make a decision. Something had to be done – and his only hope was to restore the relationship his selfish actions had destroyed. The journey to forgiveness involves a decision to make a complete change of direction that will take us back to friendship with God our Father.

A turning from the mess of the past. The way forward wasn't a matter of improving the present by patching up things as well as was possible — but by making a totally new start.

A dependence on the mercy of the Father. There was nothing the young man could do to change the situation through his own resources and power. His only hope was mercy from the one who had the ability to make the difference he needed.

An acceptance of the offer of forgiveness. When the father ran down the road to embrace him the young man gladly received all that he needed. The past was forgiven, the relationship was restored, the future was certain.

A life as a son, not a servant. The ongoing relationship was not one of duty – like a servant to a master. But of kinship – like a father and a son.

Those simple but profound steps took a young man in desperate need into the loving and permanent embrace of his father's house. It's a picture of the journey we must take if the benefit of all that Jesus did on the cross is to be ours.

The faith transaction

If you are going to claim forgiveness for yourself through an act of saving faith, just how do you go about it?

Understanding our debt

Jesus wants to wipe away our guilt and to give us a new start. And his death on the cross was to make this possible. It was as though he purchased an endless supply of forgiveness and now offers it as a completely free gift for us to receive.

Of course, that sounds unbelievable. Surely there must be something we have to do, some price we must pay, if we are to deserve such forgiveness. After all, everyone knows there's no such thing as a free lunch.

Can it really be that simple – with no strings attached? It has to be. Let me explain why no other answer is possible.

Imagine you are the world's least successful kite-flyer – the Californian whose kite hit a high-voltage power cable, caught alight and fell to the ground. The fire it started destroyed or damaged 385 houses, engulfed 740 acres of brush and caused 3,000 people to be evacuated. Total damage? Almost twenty million dollars.

Now what can you do? Will it be OK to say, 'Sorry, let me write you a cheque?' Or, 'Whoops – just leave it to me?' Just how much difference do you imagine it will make if you offer to spend your weekends helping out with a paint brush? Or living on bread and water to provide funds towards rebuilding?

Meeting that kind of overwhelming debt is totally, completely, and utterly beyond you. And then some. There's only one hope. Mercy.

In terms of our spiritual needs we are in the same mess. There is an invoice bearing our name with so many zeros it defies comprehension. Attempting to settle it from our own resources – in either cash or kind – is like trying to bail out the *Titanic* with a thimble.

Identifying our rescuer

Our only hope is mercy – which is what Jesus provides through his death on the cross. There he established the currency of forgiveness – for us to draw down and apply, by faith, to our massively overdrawn account. But this forgiveness will never be credited to our account – and so pay our debt – until we ask him to make the transfer. And this is exactly where saving faith comes in.

Let me illustrate. I get a letter from the bank telling me they are charging me £25 for informing me – in this letter – that I'm broke. Very, very, very broke. You don't need to know the gory details. But I'm in way over my head. Not only can I not pay, there's no way I will ever be able to. And to help even further, the bank tells me there will be a daily charge until I get out of debt. You've got the picture – it's going from bad to busted.

The thing is, I've got this benevolent Aunt Mabel and she's loaded – a bottomless money pit. I don't know where she got it all from – but boy, has she got it. And I need it – or at least some of it. And a note in her last Christmas card did mention that if I ever needed help I was to let her know.

So I write asking for help, owning up being unable to meet my debts. I throw myself on her mercy. And that is exactly what I receive. Aunt Mabel helps me – by arranging for a bank draft from her account to mine. When I see it there is another shock. Because not only will the payment clear my account in full but also provide me enough to guarantee me everlasting credit.

Now here is where saving faith comes in. It's not enough to recognise my need and ask for help – I have to take her at her word and present the cheque for payment. In the same way, we take hold of the blank cheque of forgiveness that Jesus created for us on the cross. We present it to God saying 'Here's payment in full.' And God says, 'You are forgiven.'

And not only is our debt wiped clear – but our spiritual account is forever treated as though it is the one belonging to Jesus himself. The bank balance of his perfect purity and sinlessness is credited to our account – for ever.

Taking the step

Have you taken that step of saving faith? Could it be you are still spiritually bankrupt – with the bailiffs at the door? If so, perhaps this is the moment for you to cash the cheque of God's forgiveness. And God is waiting to hear from you.

My communication with rich Aunt Mabel was very formal with lots of posh words. That's not what God is looking for as we come to him in saving faith. Your prayer may end up as little more than a desperate inner plea of 'help' to God. That's no problem – when you come to God in faith, he hears your words but he listens to your heart.

It may even help for you to create a picture in your mind, where you gather all the unwanted junk in your life into a huge black bin liner – or six – and put it in the hands of God in exchange for his forgiveness. Or imagine all you wish was not true about yourself as though it were a wreck of a car – crushed into a cube – and traded in for a top-of-the-range model.

If you want some words to assist you to frame what's going through your mind, the following could be appropriate. They are roughly what I said when I trusted Jesus for forgiveness:

Dear Lord God,
I am overwhelmingly in debt to you because of my sin. Because of what I am and what I have done, I have hurt you, damaged others and spoilt your world.

*I would like a new start and am now turning away from all
I know to be wrong and setting my feet on the path to follow
you.*

*Thank you that Jesus died on the cross to pay the price for
my sin. I now receive the gift of your forgiveness that this
made possible.*

*Please take hold of my life as my Lord and come and live
your life in me for ever.*

Thank you for hearing this prayer and for answering it.

Remember, such a prayer is not a magic incantation – like
wedding vows which make the event null and void if you miss
out a key sentence. Stumble and splutter all you want. Find a
quiet corner and just ache in God's presence if you must. But
you can be confident he has the resources to forgive you,
cleanse you and to fill your life with himself.

There may be barriers to believing

The decision to seize hold of God's offer of forgiveness by
faith is vastly more significant than making up your mind to
switch your brand of deodorant or to show up in church more
often. It demands even more than changing your allegiance to
a football team or taking a decision to become a vegetarian.

And weighing up a step that is this significant – letting God
rule and reign in your life – can raise all sorts of fears and
barriers. Let me just touch on a few that might be relevant.

Having to admit I'm wrong

It's been said: to err is human, to admit it is unlikely! And
seeming to lose face with those we know well can be a
sickening thought. For some who have argued that there is
no God till they are blue in the face, owning up to having
been wrong can seem hard to stomach.

But sometimes owning up to the truth is the only thing we can do and still maintain our integrity. And it's not simply about owning up that you've been driving down the motorway in the wrong direction for an hour. This is a matter of life and death.

What's worse – to look foolish, or to pass up the opportunity to be forgiven, and so become the person God created you to be?

There's still so much I don't understand

You may be thinking 'I'll jump when I know more.' But how much more will be enough? If I'd waited to gain a degree in computer engineering I'd never have splashed out on a PC and transformed the way my life operates.

I still have many unanswered questions in the IT department. But I know what I need to know – and have the daily experience of learning even more.

In some ways the step of saving faith is a lot like marriage. At some point my knowledge about Rosemary was enough for me to make an initial commitment to marry her. By saying 'I will', I gave all I knew of myself – at the time – to all I knew of her – at the time. Looking back, I now see I didn't know much about either of us.

At that point I began a progressive commitment to her – getting to know her better as my wife and discovering how much she did, in fact, love me. My understanding has grown as I've trusted in her love and our relationship has developed. But if I'd waited until I knew everything it would have been a never-ending engagement.

What I've seen puts me off

It's just possible you've seen or heard about someone who had some over-the-top experience when they became a follower of Jesus. And you'd feel really uncomfortable having to speak and believe like them. To do so just wouldn't be 'you'.

The good news is that God doesn't expect you to be anyone other than who you are. Your comfort zones are fine by him. You don't have to behave like anyone else or feel what anyone else may feel. God respects each of us for who we are – as originals, not clones.

Jesus is the only door – but it's up to you whether you come in turning cartwheels or with a dignified stride.

What will others think?

The need to hang on to our credibility in the eyes of others looms large in all our thinking. To lay ourselves open to snide remarks about having become a Jesus Freak, being away with the fairies, or retreating to the Dark Ages is no sane person's idea of fun.

Isn't it interesting that in this present tolerant, anything-goes age it is only following Jesus that evokes such comment? You can get more respect for believing in aliens, the power of crystals or claiming you're the reincarnation of Napoleon's horse trainer.

So you may well face the disdain and ridicule of others. It happened to those who first followed Jesus – and it has continued to do so ever since. And it may not stop at name calling. Many have suffered deeply for their belief in Jesus – losing their reputation, livelihood, home, family, friends and even life itself.

They made their choice based on the belief that there is nothing too great to sacrifice in order to know the forgiveness Jesus offers and the adventure that awaits us in following him.

Take your pick – respectability and popularity, or the supreme joy of forgiveness and knowing God personally through Jesus. Of course, you can have both. But don't count on it.

I'll never live up to it all

It seems such a huge step to launch out on a new relationship with Jesus. What if you severely mess up? Suppose the commitment you are thinking of making to put him first goes a bit wobbly?

The truth is you will mess up and may well graze your spiritual knees as you take your first tottering steps in following Jesus. If you don't you'll be the first. Those who follow Jesus are not perfect – just forgiven.

And God is geared up to see you through. He's there – on your side – to help you make it and to forgive you when you don't. God's a loving father, not a prison warder. He also gives you the help you are going to need – as we'll see before this book is through.

The heart of it all

The issue of saving faith is so vital I want to make it as clear as I possibly can. So imagine you are at the gates of heaven. You rub your eyes and admire your new white outfit – and move towards the doorway to wait your turn.

Ahead of you each person is being asked the same question, 'Why should God let you into his heaven?'

Up ahead you hear someone saying, 'Well, why not? I've tried my best, been nice to lots of people and never done anything really bad.'

Another responds, 'I've always helped others and am a pretty decent sort compared to most people.'

And yet another says, 'I've turned up at your place regularly and read your book and prayed a bit.'

Yet, as you watch, each one has been turned away. Because there's a problem with answers like these – however sincere they may be. And it's a big problem. If trying hard, being sincere, doing our best, and even being religious were keys that opened the door of heaven, why did Jesus have to die?

Or, to put it another way, if gaining a place in heaven can be achieved through faith in our own efforts, then the death of Jesus on the cross can only have been one huge mistake.

Please be sure this has sunk in – because it represents the heart of all this book is about. Heaven is not a place where people walk around with pride because they earned the right to be there. It's filled with those who do not deserve it, but Jesus paid the price to let them in.

And now it's your turn. 'Why should God let you into his heaven?' The only answer that brings a smile is, 'Because I have placed my faith in the sacrifice Jesus made for me on the cross.'

I hope and pray that it's yours.

Chapter 13

GRATEFUL DEAD

What could you be getting yourself into?

Did you jump? Pray the prayer? Make the vital step of saving faith? For the moment I'm assuming you didn't and you are still running in 'what am I getting myself into?' mode. And that's fine.

Yes, I do believe with every nid of my noddle that the decision in question is by far the most significant you will ever take. It's a life-changing, destiny re-routing resolution with no equal. And I'm not suggesting you should procrastinate about it.

However, spending small change takes hardly a thought. But when shelling out big time – for a car, a new audio gizmo, a holiday or whatever – I take my time over all the pros and cons. The bigger the decision, the more important it is to understand the consequences. And there's nothing bigger than this.

By the way, Jesus agrees with me – or perhaps that should be the other way round. When talking with those weighing up the prospects of following him, Jesus launched into a spiel about builders and armies. In effect he was telling them, when it comes to making up your mind, be like a builder who counts his bricks before he starts sploshing the cement;

and like a ruler who counts his soldiers before picking a fight.[1]

The message is, make sure you have what it takes. Don't end up a laughing stock – with the first few feet of your unfinished building permanently sticking out of the ground as an everlasting monument to your foolhardiness. Or like a ruler who has to live with everyone knowing he got pulverised for taking too few troops to war.

In both cases, of course, the builder and the ruler could have got it right – with a good dose of realism. And this is exactly where we are heading now. I'd like to help you weigh up all that's involved in following Jesus before you actually nail down your decision.

Naturally, if you have made the great step of saving faith – which is brilliant – you are still allowed to read on. Because there is some equally good news for you too.

A covenant commitment

Do you know what a covenant is? If I can make that clear then what follows will make so much more sense.

A covenant is a deal in which two parties say to one another 'I will if you will.' Indeed, they do more than 'say it', they pledge it. Each side promises to do their part, expecting the other side to do the same.

Some contracts come close to the concept. Take that of a professional sportsman who pledges to train, play, keep out of trouble and not mouth off to the media. While the club pledges to pay a stupid sum of money, watch over his family, keep the media off his back and stand by him if trouble comes.

The act of marriage provides an even better example of a covenant in action. In response to the bride's vows you've never heard the reply, 'That sounds like a good deal to me. Let's go and eat.'

Instead, both publicly lay out the terms of their mutual commitment to one another. They each say to the other 'I will', with every intention of doing just that. Each trusts the other will keep their vow. And this is what a covenant is all about. It's a two-sided mutually binding agreement between two willing parties.

What I'm leading you to is the fact that, throughout history, God has made a series of such covenants with his people on earth.

One such covenant was made with Moses when God gave the Ten Commandments. 'I will be your God,' said God, 'if you honour me through these commandments.' 'We will honour you through these commandments,' said the people, 'if you will be our God.'

Interestingly, the word for 'covenant' in the ancient Jewish language – Hebrew – means to cut, or to shed blood. That's where the term 'blood brothers' comes from. Two friends prick a finger smudge the blood and *voila*! 'I'm there for you and you're there for me through thick and through thin.'

Blood brothers are made through 'cutting a covenant'. In the same way God 'cut' a covenant with Israel when he gave the Commandments, except it was done through the blood of animals.

Jesus said that he came to introduce a new covenant[2] – one which was signed in his blood. Through his death, a new relationship with God became possible. Not on the basis of keeping laws and sacrificing animals – but based on the offer of free forgiveness through the death of Jesus.

Two-sided? God makes a commitment to us? Absolutely. And we'll come to all that this means in due time. But first, what is he looking for from us? If we are to turn from our self-centred, maybe very respectable but most certainly 'me'-orientated life to follow Jesus, what is our side of the bargain?

I hope you are ready for a shock . . .

The job description is 'Disciple'

Let me take you to Jesus' recruitment office. There's a sign on the door saying 'Disciples Wanted'.

The word 'disciple' is a close equivalent to what we call an 'apprentice'. The vacant position doesn't carry a mega-salary with all the perks. Instead, the working conditions promise an early start, long days, a minimum wage for a menial task and a prove-your-worth-by-keeping-on commitment.

Jesus was not out to gather the largest possible fan club. Instead of admirers he was after disciples. To him, the argument 'Ten thousand people can't be wrong' meant nothing. Small could be beautiful if it was a genuine group dedicated to all he stood for.

Jesus knew people had a whole bunch of self-motivated reasons for following him. Some would just crave the excitement. Others the buzz of something new. Others would see it as a way to power and significance for themselves. And, for some, the thought of free food for ever – even if it was only bread and fish – was motive enough.

He is not after volunteers, do-gooders and those who think 'aren't you fortunate to have me among your number'. He is after those who, like an apprentice, will spend most of their time learning. They don't yet know much – but they know a man who does and are following him.

But what about all this stuff about counting bricks and soldiers? What is it that being a disciple of Jesus lets us in for, that may be beyond our resources?

As you saunter through the door of this mythical recruitment office you are confronted with posters that cover the walls. Each is emblazoned with one of the 'come follow me' slogans Jesus used to the crowds that came to hear him. You're about to get the picture.

A disciple is ready to give up his own life

The first to catch your eye is subtle in the extreme. 'Anyone who does not carry his cross and follow me cannot be my disciple'.[3]

Those who heard Jesus say these words knew exactly what he had in mind. It was a common sight to see those branded as criminals making their journey towards death with the equipment for their execution on their back. One day, Jesus would do the same.

There was no mistaking his message.

Discipleship is a public issue. Don't think about following me unless you're ready to own me publicly, Jesus was saying. And remember, there may be more shame than gain.

In most societies of the world it is simply not cool to be a disciple. You can get away with being nice in his name, joining the Christian club or dipping your toe in the water a little. But become a genuine disciple and your street-cred rating could plunge to zilch.

Suddenly you are at odds with the values and attitudes of a selfish me-centred society. You stick out like a very sore thumb. Not that you go looking for it. You don't have to. You just find most people are swimming in the opposite direction. They are dressed for leisure and you have your fatigues on.

And Jesus says, unless you are ready for that you are not ready to follow me.

Discipleship is a life and death issue. Those who carried their cross counted themselves as already dead. They had no plans for anything else. In the same way, Jesus calls us to die to our own selfishness, vain ambitions and personal priorities.

The approach Jesus takes is in stark contrast to the advertising once used to recruit soldiers for the British army. Integrity would have meant a headline offering 'Come and die for Queen and country.' Instead a more palatable message appeared with an almost holiday-brochure feel. The invitation? 'Join the army and see the world.'

Jesus is far more honest. But not too honest for our own good. He wants us to know exactly what we are getting into. With no false expectancy, no illusions, and no bargains.

Don't follow Jesus to find fulfilment – though I guarantee you'll find it. Don't follow Jesus for excitement – yet it will never be in short supply. Instead follow Jesus to 'die'. And sometimes this can be true in real terms.

Many of the first followers of Jesus lived under Roman rule. The emperor was thought of as God, and at times they were forced to worship him – by hailing him as Lord and making a sacrifice at an altar to his name. Refusal meant death.

So why not worship the emperor? It was only an outward act and God would understand. But they were disciples and knew such an act would deny everything they stood for. There could only be one God and one Lord and ruler of their lives. No price was too great for them to pay. Thousands of them paid it. And have gone on doing so – in different settings throughout history.

Following Jesus means counting ourselves as dead to all that feeds our self-centredness. Because he matters more than life itself. In fact, he *is* life itself.

We follow Jesus on his terms or not at all – as the following, adapted from an anonymous author, sums up perfectly.

Here I am, Jesus. You said 'Take up your cross,' and I'm here to do it. I'll bet you wish more people were willing to be disciples like me. I've counted the cost and surrendered my life, and it's not an easy road.

What crosses do you have on offer? I'm not fussy, you understand. But I'd kind of like one with a bit of style. You need disciples who are relevant.

I was wondering, are there any that are vinyl padded? There's no point being uncomfortable and you'd get more recruits that way.

Or is there one that packs flat – Ikea style? Then I can tuck it under my coat at difficult moments. You wouldn't want me to ever get embarrassed would you?

Funny, there doesn't seem to be much choice here. Just that coarse, rough wood. I mean that would hurt. Don't you have something more distinctive? None of my friends are going to be impressed by this shoddy workmanship. They'll think I'm odd or something. And so will my family.

What's that? It's either one of these or forget the whole thing? But Jesus, I want to be your disciple. Just being with you; that's all that counts. But you don't understand – nobody lives that way today! Start getting radical like this, and they'll start examining my head for bumps.

Following you could have a lot going for it. And I want to do it. But I do have some rights, you know. Now let's see. Jesus? Jesus?

Now where do you suppose he went?

A disciple is ready to say goodbye to everything

Eyes to the left and another poster hits you: 'Any of you who does not give up everything cannot be my disciple.'[4] Eyes to the right and there's another. 'If anyone comes to me and does not hate his father and mother, his wife and children, his brothers and sisters yes, even his own life he cannot be my disciple'.[5]

This isn't what you had expected. Where's the red carpet? And the 'we sure do need you' customer care attitude you feel you deserve? Well, you were warned.

But surely Jesus doesn't want you to sell everything down to your underwear and for good measure to launch a hate campaign on those you love the most. You're right, he doesn't.

Jesus is using a style of Jewish speech that exaggerates something to the point of unreality to drive home a point. He did much the same with stories about people who had planks in their eyes and camels going through the eyelet hole of a needle.

But the points he makes are still big ones. He wants would-be disciples to understand two more vital things.

He's more important than anything we own. There is nothing worth clinging on to if it keeps us from following him. That's the message.

Disciples are asked to have the same attitude to life as their master. Jesus owned heaven and all its splendour. But, for our sake, he chose to die to all that it offered. Instead of clinging on to his rights as God, he willingly became a man, humbling himself to die on a cross.

Jesus, who was rich beyond all our understanding, became poor so that we who are bankrupt could have his riches. All he had in his hands were the nails our sin put there.

When what we own conflicts with following him, there is only one choice on offer.

He's more important than anyone we know. We are to love him so much it would almost seem to others that they were hated.

Let me allow Joseph Steinberg to describe what this meant for him. He puts it this way:

In the Jewish home where I grew up, my family and I were very close. My relationships were so fulfilling – especially with my parents. We loved each other so, so much.

Then, at the time when a young man and a father are growing closer – I became a believer in Jesus. I didn't realise just how this would impact the life of our family – especially the relationship with my father. When I finally got the nerve to tell them about my decision it didn't go down too well – it seemed my new-found faith especially hurt him.

Of course, I wasn't trying to cause anyone pain. It's just that I couldn't deny I'd met a real, living person, whom I knew to be the Messiah I'd always longed for. I suppose my love for Jesus could have been mistaken for an act of rebellion towards my parents or a hatred of my Jewish upbringing. But it wasn't.

It was just that I now had a very real relationship with the living God – something I could not, with all integrity, deny. I'm sure I could have handled it all more sensitively. But what had once been a close, sharing relationship with my father, became one of a strained silence for a number of years – causing great sadness for both of us.

Joseph had a choice to make. A costly one. And Jesus warns us that following him may demand the same for us.

Following Jesus is not about patronising his causes, cleaning up our act somewhat or showing our face more often on a Sunday. It's about putting our whole life under his control and making him the ultimate ruler of all we are, say, and do.

How this may work out will be very different for each of us. But the principle remains constant. To be a disciple means only the best will do. In God's terms, our very best is ourselves – all we are and all we have – made totally available to him.

A disciple is one who is obedient

Look left again and there's another poster on the wall. 'If you love me, you will do as I command'.[6]

That's plain enough. Love and obedience, Jesus wants us to know, go hand in hand. The two are inseparable.

That word 'obey' probably evokes an image of dog training and obedience classes – and Jesus demanding we stop at the kerb and respond to the command 'leap'. I can't help that – but it's a far from accurate picture.

What it means is that a disciple of Jesus salutes his flag, marches to his commands and checks out his orders of the day – and then does them.

An essential ingredient in a covenant is that both parties work for their mutual benefit. Sportsman and club, husband and wife, are to act only in the best interests of the other.

'Jump,' I yelled. And Rosemary jumped. Just in time to avoid the falling branch. She knew me well enough to know I wasn't playing games and that she wouldn't land in a pile of dog deposit. Though, to be honest, there was a time I told her to lick 'ice cream' off a spoon when it was actually horseradish. But that was just for fun.

Being a disciple is not a matter of listening to the words of Jesus or even applauding them. Disciples listen and act. What could that involve?

Jesus spoke about forgiving those who wrong us, turning the other cheek, praying for those who are unkind to us; not fretting about how things will work out, and avoiding public display when we help others. He spoke of our need to be meek, merciful, pure in heart, and people who seek after peace. And a lot more besides.

He added that someone who failed to put his words into practice was like an incompetent buffoon who built his house on sand. So when the storms of life came – whammo. While the wise builder – the disciple – put them into practice, giving their life a solid a foundation.

Having looked so fully at what our side of the agreement involves, it's almost time to see all that God has for us as his part of the covenant. I can't wait to tell you. But first, one very important thing.

Behaving like a disciple doesn't get you to heaven

It's important you don't misread me. There is no merit in doing all the things a disciple does unless you have first made a faith commitment to Jesus.

Yes, the world will be a marginally better place if you act like a disciple. But no, it won't make you any more qualified for heaven than you are already. Being a disciple is not part of the journey towards the cross – it's the road that leads on from there. Indeed, the contrast could not be greater.

If you try to behave like a disciple of Jesus in order to gain forgiveness, you face a miserable uphill climb that heads right off a precipice. You can grit your teeth and obey everything Jesus taught, do everything he tells us to do and abandon everything you possess, but you will still remain unforgiven. Because forgiveness is a gift we can never earn.

To reach the door of forgiveness, all you can carry with you is regret for the past and trust in the sacrifice Jesus made on the cross for your sin. Once through the door your discipleship journey begins and it is far more downhill than you may ever imagine – as you are about to read.

Chapter 14

MATHEMATICAL CERTAINTY

Does the other side of the equation add up?

The tune is not on my personal play list but the sentiment is right on the knuckle. Here we go, one, two, three – *'All of me. Why not take all of me.'*

Who do I have in mind to be singing it? You? After all we've just been looking at you probably think so. But no. God is the vocalist – and I know he will mean every word.

This is his part of the pact. His side of the covenant. As our blood brother he says, 'Not only do I want all of you. But you get all of me.'

What a deal. And how we need him.

No hope for loners

Think back to all that's expected of us as disciples. Does it all sound hard? How about 'impossible'? You're right. Absolutely. To be the kind of faithful follower of Jesus that he asks us to be is quite outside our human ability.

Left to our own resources we don't have it in us to love God and our neighbour with everything we've got. Or the inner strength to be the person God desires, and to fulfil the plans he has for us.

152

So that's it then, is it? We've put our head above the parapet and decided it's not nice out there. Let's pack up the tent and go home. Not a bit of it. Because God has the answer – himself.

He is our resource for the journey

This is why God wants us to take all of him. Because it is all of him we need. Jesus calls us to follow him. We say 'yes'. God says, 'You'll never make it without the right equipment. And I'm the equipment you'll need.'

Have you ever watched a TV programme on ocean racing or some epic journey to the frozen north? Then you'll have seen the vast quanity of provisions stored on the boat or on the sleds. Every conceivable cranny gets stuffed with nourishing things. The provisions are built in at the very start of the design process, because they are essential to the team's success.

Our journey as disciples will be every bit as hazardous and demanding and God can give us all the equipment we need for our journey – himself.

To put it simply, when we make that saving faith commitment to God he does not say, 'Nice one. Make sure you keep it up.' Instead he greets us with, 'I'm going to come and live in you and change you from the inside out.

Writing to those who were followers of Jesus, one of the first Christian leaders put it like this. 'The Spirit of him who raised Jesus from the dead is living in you.'[1] The same writer explained that God had 'put his Spirit in our hearts'.[2]

Who and what is he talking about? About the creator God – living in us. Why? Because we need the power of God within us if we are to live a life that pleases him. As the same early Christian leader put it, 'God will strengthen us with power in our inner being'.[3]

As we journey onward from that door of forgiveness,

God's not encouraging us from the sidelines – like a parent at a school sports day. Enthusiastic, caring, but powerless. Instead, he's actually running in our shoes.

I remember watching my son Joel zoom round a racing track at the wheel of a high-powered sports car. The experience was an eighteenth birthday gift. I was impressed – until his instructor changed places with him and took control. Then we saw what could be done and the motoring really began. But it was only possible because the one who could make the difference was in the driving seat.

And that's where we need God to be at work. Within us. At the very heart of all we are. And for three good reasons.

They're out to get us

Think of it like this. You're a hollow tin ball being used for the squash championship of life. I know squash balls aren't made of tin, but humour me. And there are three finalists putting you through the school of hard knocks.

Finalist number one – the world. He's a crowd pleaser and wants to entice you to be one too. Subtlety is his strength – full of flicks and drop shots. No wonder he's world champion.

Most people dance to his tune and he wants to trap you into doing the same. To have the same values and attitudes as the great multitude of God-ignorers out there. He mutters as he whacks you with his racket, 'Forget God and do what everyone else is doing – just keep on bouncing, bouncing.'

And the temptation is great to do just that.

Finalist number two – the flesh. The name doesn't sound very nice – and he isn't. He's a pig of a player. Plays dirty, breaks the rules, and has to – because he's not much good at what he does. He's constantly out of control – and leaves a trail of mess and destruction behind wherever he goes.

He's your own inner nature – which infects all you do with a tendency towards pride and a belief you can do it all yourself. He'll trip you up time and time again.

What makes him one of the more devastating players is that he has the ability to blame his faults on others. The opponent, the referee, the crowd, his potty training. He may look good – but he is rotten to the core. He will rot you from the inside out and take you down.

Finalist number three – the Devil. Forget pictures of pitch-fork, horns, and spiky tail – this guy looks great. Mister 'lean and agile' – with the smug smile of a used car salesman. Don't underestimate his power to hit you out of the court – he's fast, fit and furious.

He has no end of schemes up his tee shirt to keep you bouncing around – dented and distracted from thinking about God forever. His smash is devastating. And he just keeps on coming at you – especially when you are not expecting it.

These three enemies are what make following Jesus impossible under your own steam. And as they put your life as a tin squash ball through its paces you'll get a real beating. Long before your four-score years are up you will look more like a cheese grater than a squash ball. Dented, dinged, damaged, and drilled through with holes from bends, breaks, and bad bounces.

That's why we need God to come in with his strength and power. How different the game would be if your tin shell was fortified with a solid new core – that filled you and pushed out all the dents and dings.

And that's what God wants to do – pour his presence into you like molten steel. And so transform you into something entirely new – restored to a perfection better than when you were first created, and with a perfect bounce.

That whole tin squash ball routine is a daft picture. But it expresses the astounding truth that, when we trust Jesus, for forgiveness God makes us an entirely different person on the inside.

Back to the factory

But why are we born as hollow tin balls in the first place – instead of burly ball bearings? Wouldn't that have been better?

Jesus explained the reason why to a great religious leader named Nicodemus. The man was one of the more respected rule keepers of Jesus' day and sincerely wanted to know God better.

Jesus said some radical things to him. And he also says them to us. So imagine you're sitting there face to face with Jesus – needing the same answers.

You say, 'Jesus, you know I try to play by all the rules. I'm pretty OK – and yet there is something missing at the very centre of my life. Can you help me?'

Jesus says to you, 'You've had that problem since you were born. And it's one you never noticed.'

'You see,' he continues, 'when you were born you were physically alive and fine. But there was a major problem at your birth. Your spirit was still-born. Though your body was alive your spirit was dead to me. Your disease called sinfulness means your spiritual heart did not start beating and it hasn't started yet.'

The only answer, Jesus explains, is to be born spiritually in the same way you were physically. Having been born from the womb you now need to be born from the Spirit.[4]

If you are to come alive to God you must allow him to place a new spirit within you – his Spirit. In doing so he creates for us all what was done for that imaginary tin squash ball – only more.

Imagine a shape like our English letter Y. If it had no centre it would simply fall apart. Our lives are like that – falling apart without God filling our birth defect, the spiritual hole in our heart.

God's plan is to make us completely new people. To give us a totally new operating system – free of the bugs and corrupt files we were born with. He gives us a brand new hard disk and downloads everything we need – in the form of himself.

God in three persons

To help you grasp the immensity of what it means to have all that God is on our side and within us, I need to unpack what it means for God to be a trinity. This is slightly technical stuff. But it's worth it – because there's even more to God than you have yet to discover.

You'll have heard the word Trinity. Or phrases like 'the Holy Trinity – Father, Son and Holy Spirit.' And probably been as confused as most people. It's not a word Jesus ever used and neither did his earliest followers. But gradually it became a useful way of identifying what they all knew to be true.

The issue is this. While there is but one God, he is three persons – God the Father, God the Son and God the Holy Spirit. All are equal. All are the same. All have different roles and functions. They are inseparably separate. They are at one and *are* one – yet they are three.

There – it's clear as mud! So try it this way:

- God is God – and Jesus spoke of him as Father.[5]
- Jesus is God – and God spoke of him as 'my son'.[6]
- The Holy Spirit is God – which is the way Jesus spoke of him.[7]

For centuries the early disciples used a symbol shaped like our English letter Y to remind them of all that God is and to help them understand the concept of God as Trinity. Three prongs – but one letter. Three persons – but one God.

Those who knew Jesus and followed him came to be in no doubt that both Jesus and the Holy Spirit were God, as much as the Father was God. And they constantly spoke of the three in the same breath – just as Jesus had done.

So how come, if there are three persons who are God, we can still talk about there being only one God? Surely there must be three? After all, the maths is easy: $1+1+1 = 3$.

But try the sum this way: $1 \times 1 \times 1 = ?$ Right – One!

It is this three-person God who invests himself in us.

The Father – the perfect parent

Jesus told his followers to speak to God as 'our Father'.[8] And Jesus himself used the word 'Abba' – a Hebrew word meaning Daddy[9] – in conversation with his Father in heaven. And there was hardly a more intimate word in his vocabulary than the one toddlers first utter while hugged in their father's embrace.

The startling good news is that God becomes your Father when you come to him in faith for forgiveness and are born spiritually.

Of course, in human terms fathers are a mixed bag. I'm not everything my kids hope for and deserve – nor was my own father. But God is the perfect parent. He is everything we wish our human parents had been and more.

He's always there for us, always has time, always does what is in our best interest. And as the one with inexhaustible supplies of everything – he has a bottomless well of love, patience, compassion and fairness.

He loves us no matter what. The mark of a true parent is to love and keep on loving. No matter how wayward and rebellious any of my kids may turn out to be, I'd like to believe there's nothing they could ever do to stop me loving them.

This is even more true with God. His love is strong enough for him to sacrifice his son for us. And it's the foundation of our whole relationship with him.

He's at work on our behalf. Ask your heavenly Father for whatever you need, said Jesus, and you will get it. Of course, there's a considerable gap between what we want and what we really need. And God's assessment of our need can be different again from ours.

As a loving Father, God listens and answers – with our very best interests always on his heart. But of course, it's those who know him as Father who are invited to pray 'our Father'. There's a vast difference between my children asking me for something and their friends making the same request.

My kids get special treatment and so do we.

The Son – the image of the Father

When Jesus left the earth at the end of his resurrection appearances his work was not over.

He holds us in his grasp. 'No one can snatch my sheep from my grasp,' Jesus promised his disciples. The hands that created the universe – the same hands that were staked to the cross – now hold us firmly in their grasp. No matter how many times we fall or fail, Jesus has us safe and secure.

With a toddler in tow across a busy street we hold hands. At least, that's what it looks like. In reality, that little hand is firmly encased in one which will never let it go. And that is how secure

Jesus keeps us when we commit ourselves to follow him. His love will never let us slip from his grasp.

The Holy Spirit – our helper

You may think it doesn't look as though Jesus is doing a whole lot now that his work on earth is finished. Yes and no. He has a lot to do – but he's delegated!

Just before he was arrested – and the journey towards crucifixion began – Jesus made a promise to his disciples that he would send them a replacement for himself – one who would be everything they needed to be his disciples.[10] He would send them the Holy Spirit.

Their job was to live God's way and to turn others to the same path. Yet Jesus, the one who was the very centre of their lives, was leaving them. They needed something – or someone – special.

Jesus told them they would be drenched or submerged in the Holy Spirit – like a sunken boat which has water inside and out. As the disciples said 'yes' to God by giving themselves to him, God would say 'yes' to them by filling them with his presence and power.

As he spoke to them, Jesus made it clear that the Holy Spirit would be everything those who followed him needed after he had gone.

The Holy Spirit is our constant helper. As Jesus' time on earth was ending, he promised to send his Holy Spirit so every disciple would have him with them all of the time, wherever they were.

Today, God lives in each true follower of Jesus through his Holy Spirit – including you if you trust him by faith. He will be with you all the time and in every situation – no matter how demanding or difficult. Seven days a week.

The Holy Spirit reminds us of what we hear. There's a super-natural dimension to learning and understanding the truth about God – and the Holy Spirit makes it happen. Through his help we remember more of what we have heard and learned about him than we would have thought possible.

It's remarkable. Time and again, when I need it, some aspect of what I've heard or learned about God suddenly pops into my brain from I know not where – except that I do know where. The Holy Spirit is at work.

The three of us who worked on this book together would tell you that without the helper Jesus sent, this book could not have been written. Time and again we have wondered if we would have the right thing to say at the right moment. And it was, brought to our memory by the Holy Spirit in us.

He will do exactly the same for you if you trust him too.

The Holy Spirit teaches us what we need to learn. The Holy Spirit opens our understanding to the truth about God. Which is how uneducated people like the first disciples made such an impact.

The limit to what God can teach you and do through you is not your memory, intelligence or education. It is your willingness to allow the Holy Spirit to teach you.

I've lost count of the times I've seen people say 'now I see it' about some vital issue concerning God's message to us. And it's been much more than the penny dropping. Instead, God by his Spirit had done what he promised – opened their mind to what is true about him.

If a lot of what I'm talking about in this book makes as much sense as Alphabet Spaghetti, don't panic. The Holy Spirit is ready to make it clear to you – as he has down through the ages to millions of others.

The Holy Spirit gives us the power we need. What was going
to transform a group of frightened and very ordinary people
into those who would go on to turn the world upside down?
It was not will power. It was the power of the living God
within them.

That power is an inner strength to be and do what's simply
not possible through our own abilities. It includes:

- having courage beyond our expectations in difficult
  situations
- finding the strength to go on when humanly we've run
  out of road
- developing a character like that of Jesus himself –
  through the qualities of love, patience, self-control, joy,
  serenity and so on growing in our lives
- receiving special abilities – a few or many – to use in the
  service of God, his people, and the world: from being
  better able to explain more clearly what we believe, to
  being great at administration or hospitality; from the
  ability to worship him with all we've got, to the strength
  to die for him if it comes to it.

On the fence at the end of my neighbours' garden – the nice
neighbours who don't have a dog that wakes us up in the early
hours – is a 'plastic man with a windmill thing'. The man
holds a crank handle which is joined to the windmill. And
when the wind blows, the windmill turns and the man cranks.

Except that it looks to be the other way round. At first
sight, it appears that the man is doing all the work. That's
how it is when the Holy Spirit is at work in us. He does the
work and we get to look good.

Without the Holy Spirit's presence, a disciple of Jesus
would be like a sail without the wind. The Holy Spirit makes
following Jesus possible.

The Holy Spirit helps us be sure we are God's child. Perhaps, above all else, you wonder how you could possibly know God has heard and answered your prayer for his forgiveness and new life.

Maybe you have prayed such a prayer and you didn't hear the angels break out into the Hallelujah Stomp. Or maybe you did – and are confused.

Again, this is where the Holy Spirit goes to work. One of the most wonderful things he does is to help us know, deep within us, that we have been forgiven and are now God's child.

Of course, that step of saving faith happens in different ways for different people. For some it is a very dramatic moment. They can tell you exactly when and where it took place and even the colour of the wallpaper in the room at the time.

Others, like me, find they gradually reach a point where they can look back and realise they are trusting in Jesus and not themselves for their future with God.

Some are as cool as a cucumber. Others weep buckets. My daughter Xanna asked me, 'Does it tickle a bit when you ask Jesus to come into your life?' because for her it had. Others just have a great sense of relief over having finally settled the matter.

I picture it like crossing the equator. Some mark the moment with great ceremony and a glass of bubbly. Others look back only to realise it has already happened. But both have passed from one side of the world to the other.

When it comes to being sure, whatever your experience – or lack of one – several things remain true.

- You will begin to see signs of change in your life – old attitudes will start to go and new desires begin to grow. In effect you'll begin acting like a butterfly instead of a caterpillar.
- What you hear about God will increasingly make sense – and you'll grow hungry for more.

- You will start to experience a deep inner peace.
- You'll see the world with clearer eyes and a fresh perspective. Life will take on a quality that you had never thought possible.

But far above anything that may or may not happen to you, remember one thing. God can be trusted to keep his promises. You may not feel different, but that does not change the fact that God had promised you his forgiveness if you ask for it and will keep his word.

Whether or not I feel married doesn't make an inch of difference to what's true. Two people said 'yes' and that settled it. If you've said 'yes' to God and meant it he has most definitely said 'yes' to you.

Finally, there's one great test. Can you say with conviction – 'Jesus is the Lord of my life'? When you can, you know you have become God's child through faith in his son.

A final chorus

You've looked at the challenge of what being a disciple of Jesus means. You've seen the wonderful commitment God makes of himself to provide all you require and more.

So could it be the time to burst into song? With God and you singing in perfect harmony. *'All of me. Why not take all of me.'*

Or, make it a prayer along the lines of: *'Here I am with all my sin, doubts, failure and confusion. I'm trusting in Jesus' death on the cross for me. Please take me as I am and make me what you want me to be. Clean me up from inside out and fill me with everything you are.'*

Or you may want to flick back to the prayer on page 135 of this book to make your commitment. There is an adventure waiting.

Chapter 15

THE GAME OF LIFE

Is it OK for rules to rule?

Jesus said – no doubt with a big smile on his face – 'I came so that everyone would have life, and have it in its fullest.'[1] He was speaking to those who were his followers. And he meant it. Just like everything else he ever said.

Yet you may well be expecting something very different from 'life' and 'fullest' as you look into the future as a follower of Jesus. Did you see the next step as taking delivery of the book, *Two Hundred Ways to Keep God Happy, Vol. 1*, bound nicely in black? And the prospect of a joyless drudgery of keeping rules.

Why do we so easily get it wrong about following Jesus? An incident involving a good friend of mine illustrates it perfectly. Jeff Lucas often speaks about God at large conferences. At one such event – held at a holiday complex where there was maid service for the chalets where he was staying – life became very 'interesting'.

One morning, he was on his way between bathroom and bedroom, stark naked, when a cleaning maid burst helpfully on the scene. Jeff recalls, 'She looked me in the eye – for which I was most grateful – and asked unfalteringly, "Would you like clean bed linen?"'

Despite the bizarre circumstances her oft-repeated lines never wavered – even in the presence of a man of the cloth totally in the buff. She did what she had always done – read the script.

It's easy to fall into the same trap when it comes to following Jesus. We assume it's all about locking ourselves into a routine and nailing down a set of rules and expectations. Lots of them. And sticking to them.

We treat following Jesus as though we are playing some great new board game. Where we open the box and – first things first – read the rules. Before we know where we are we've stacked up loads of them. Things we must do, ought to do, dare not do, feel compelled to do – if we are to keep God happy.

None of this sounds much like 'life in its fullest' no matter how it is packaged. So how can we achieve what Jesus had in mind?

There is nothing we can do to earn God's love

The first thing is to be absolutely clear about the basis of our relationship with God.

The world over, people imagine the only way they can relate to God is through the things they do. By being good enough often enough they'll pass.

The first step to saving faith is to understand how wrong this is – and that only the goodness of Jesus can meet our needs. So what is it that changes after we put our faith in Jesus and have begun to follow him? Nothing! Our goodness still doesn't match up.

Just as we couldn't earn points with God before we were forgiven, we can't earn them now. There is still nothing we can do to earn God's favour and cause him to love us more. His love is at full stretch already.

I love the way this is expressed by the Brooklyn Jewish playwright, Paddy Chayefsky, in his play *Gideon*. There's a scene in which Gideon is out in the desert in his tent a thousand miles from nowhere, feeling deserted and rejected by God.

One night, God breaks into the tent and Gideon is overcome, burnt by the wild fire of God's love. He is up all night, pacing back and forth in his tent.

Finally dawn comes, and Gideon – in his Brooklyn Jewish accent – cries out, 'God, oh God, all night long I've thought of nuttin' but you, nuttin' but you. I'm caught up in the raptures of love. God, I want to take you into my tent, wrap you up, and keep you all to myself. God, hey God, tell me that you love me.'

God answers, 'I love you, Gideon.'

'Yeh, tell me again, God.'

'I love you, Gideon.'

Gideon scratches his head. 'I don't understand. Why? Why do you love me?'

And God scratches his head and answers, 'I really don't know. Sometimes, Gideon, my passion is unreasonable.'

And that's it. God's love for you is unreasonable. It always has been and always will be. It was his unreasonable love that sent Jesus to the cross for you. It is his unreasonable love that continues to burn for you, no matter what.

God loved you unreasonably at the time you spurned his love. And he is just as unreasonable now that you have surrendered to him.

There's nothing you can do to make God love you more than he does already. Nothing. God's love can't be earned. We have never deserved it and will never deserve it. But he loves us anyway. Because that's the kind of God he is. He just keeps on loving. It's his nature.

Even kids know that you can never force anyone to love

you. Either you are loved or you are not. Keeping rules or not keeping rules will never change how God feels about you. He loves you – he just can't help himself. He even likes you.

If only we would sit still long enough to grasp the deep, deep heartfelt passion that God has for each of us. Then perhaps we could see that we can never work hard enough to deserve God's love.

Instead we might even relax and bask in that love in the way God intends us to.

Rules are not God's plan

God hates man-made rules that just involve duty.

When Jesus was on earth the Pharisees – the religious lawmakers – had cornered the market in rule-making and policing law-breaking. They had hundreds of petty rules, like how much you could greet a bride on her wedding day and how much you could console a widow at her funeral. To keep them was like trying to pat your head, rub your belly, do a somersault, flip a pancake and tie your shoes – all at the same time.

Catch this – there were even rules about what kind of rope you could use to lower a bucket into a well on the day of rest, the 'Sabbath'. The verdict was you couldn't use rope, as this would constitute work. But the rules did allow you to tie your bra as that was necessary for modesty. So you could tie a bra to a bucket and get water from the well that way.

We can find ourselves heading in the same direction. From the sincerest of motives we try to earn God's love and forgiveness by religiously keeping a set of rules.

Jesus used the strongest language to denounce these kind of shenanigans. The Pharisees caught the sharp edge of his tongue because of the way they tied the people up in knots –

or bra straps – with the endless petty rules they gave out for pleasing God.

You can easily understand why.

Rule-keeping is based on pride. In keeping rules, Jesus said, the Pharisees were trusting in their own ability to earn God's love, rather than resting in the passionate love God had for them all the time. They foolishly believed they had something to contribute to the equation. It's the same for us.

Rule-keeping rejects God's love. Imagine how you would feel if, time after time, the person you loved so deeply never accepted it. Instead if they continually behaved like an obsessive-compulsive idiot in order to try and make you love them – when you already did.

When Jesus calls out to us in love, it is not to a whole new set of rules, but to a whole new way of life – a life of rest from the inner struggle to earn love.

If not rules, what?

When Jesus set out his plan for those who follow him he made no mention of the compulsory wearing of open-toed sandals and singing 'Kumbaya'. Instead he spoke of our goal as to 'Love the Lord God with all your heart, soul, mind and strength and love your neighbour as yourself'.[2]

That's a pretty broad and exciting landscape to be travelling over. It involves putting the best interest of God and others at the top of our priorities – and doing so with energy and enthusiasm.

A living relationship

Instead of rules, God has called us to a relationship with him. Let me explain it this way. The ushers have asked each guest, 'Are you with the gride or the broom?' And the happy couple are ready to exchange their vows before the assembled multitude.

You can hardly believe your ears. 'Do you, Cedric, promise never to leave your toenail cuttings on the bedroom floor, always to empty the kitchen pedal bin, always to rinse round the bath after you've used it, never to do the crossword when it's not your turn, always to put the toilet seat down again when you've finished, to say please and thank you in a cheery voice even when you have toothache, to . . .' The vows that follow, from Gladys, are equally detailed and rule-based.

You've never heard anything like it. Because the basis for marriage is not rules but a relationship – with the significant commitments to honour, worship, obey, cherish, share, and so on.

In the same way, this is what God has in mind for us. He wants a relationship based on our mutual needs and expectations. A relationship where we get to know him better, understand his ways more clearly, and live accordingly.

It reminds me of the woman who was married to a demanding perfectionist. He made endless lists of things he wanted her to do. And she tried her best to accomplish them. When she failed – as she often did – her husband got mad, became cold and denied her his affection.

Eventually the man died – probably from an over-active misery gland – and the woman remarried. Her second husband was utterly different. She deserved better and got it. He was loving, supportive and never demanded a thing.

One day, rummaging through some old papers, she came across a list of expectations from husband number one. To her amazement she found she was doing all this and more for her new man – but not because he demanded it. Her actions were an unconscious response to his love.

We can all too easily imagine that God is like that first

rule-giving, task-inflicting husband. And that our only hope is to earn his love.

When, actually, God is like the second husband – the one who loves us no matter what. And does so fully and completely with the result that we find ourselves responding instinctively to all that he is – because of the relationship we have with him.

Accepted as we are

So what about those things we feel we 'ought' to do because they will improve our relationship with God? Where do rules come in here?

Let me give you an example. Let's say you agree with God that, at a specific time each day, you'll spend some time alone focusing on him in your thoughts and with the aid of the Bible. That's not a bad idea, but there are two ways you can approach this commitment.

You can say, 'I will spend time with God like this because he loves me and I love him and it's great to talk.' Or you can say, 'I'm going to do this to make sure he will keep on loving me, and because I know others who do it and feel I ought to.'

It's the motive behind keeping these 'rules' that's important.

This means it is not our duty to meet with others who follow Jesus. It's our joy – because it's great to be with those who are as grateful for God's love as we are.

It's not our duty to pray – it's just brilliant to be able to talk to the one who loves us so much. It's not our duty to tell others the good news about Jesus – it's something that just happens when you have had such love lavished on you.

What about when we fail?

There will be many times when we don't live up to our goals and aspirations. And there's nothing to feel guilty about when that happens – unless others get hurt in the process. It's OK to aim for the stars and hit the moon. Or to plan to read the whole Bible in a year and only get halfway. This is not something to feel deeply guilty about.

But there will be times when our failure is actually sin. Because, despite our growing desire to love God and others, there will be times when we don't. Our deep-rooted human pride and selfishness will see to that. And what then?

The answer revolves round the two kinds of relationship that we have with God if we have come to him in saving faith. Two? Yes, two.

The two relationships I have with God are like the two relationships I have with any one of my five children. First there's the legal relationship – by birth. And there is nothing they or I can do to change it.

In the same way, through faith in Jesus, we become adopted by God as his child. As John put it in his gospel, 'To all who received him (Jesus), to those who believed in his name, he gave the right to become the children of God'.[3] That relationship is irreversible and unbreakable too – no matter what you may do.

The other father and child relationship I have is exactly that – a parental relationship. It can be close and intimate. Or strained and even broken. But all the time our legal relationship remains intact.

What it means, for example, is had one of my offspring hurled a bowl of cornflakes across the breakfast table at me they would have still been my child – but it wouldn't have been a good moment to ask for a new bike for Christmas.

That is how it can be with us, as God's children. From the moment when saving faith transforms our relationship with God, we become his child. And that legal relationship can never change. But there are times when our wilful or thoughtless behaviour makes him sad, gives us a sense that we're no longer in his presence, and robs us of the enjoyment of the privileges we enjoy as God's child.

What we need is a way back. And God has made it possible.

Restoring the relationship

If ever you think you've slipped so far from God's love that you can never come back, think of one of Jesus' best friends – the disciple, Peter. He made more of a mess of things than you could imagine.

Peter and Jesus were great friends. So close they were that, when Jesus said all his friends would one day deny they knew him, Peter protested, 'No way, Lord. I will die with you before I deny you.' But Jesus said, 'You will deny me Peter – even three times before the cock crows in the morning.'

Within hours Jesus was arrested and Peter, who was by his side, ran off. Then, as he sneaked back to follow events, three different people recognised Peter as a follower of Jesus. Three times he lied to deny that he knew Jesus or had ever had anything to do with him. And his language was not pretty.

But now, three strikes and Peter was out. The cock crowed. Jesus turned and looked right into Peter's eyes. And Peter fled and wept bitterly.

That was far from the end of the story. The time came when, soon after Jesus rose from the dead, that the two again came face to face. Peter may have expected a full-scale rebuke. But all he received was love.[4]

It happened by the side of a lake after Peter and his fellow disciples had been fishing all night. The risen Jesus called him from the beach. Recognising the voice, Peter swam ashore, where Jesus had cooked fish for breakfast. Then Jesus asked, 'Peter, do you love me?'

As Peter warmed his hands round the fire in the cold morning air, probably his mind flashed back to the fire he had sat by while he denied he knew Jesus – just a few days ago. As he did so, Peter really had to face up to his betrayal.

In that setting Jesus gently asked him three times, 'Do you love me?' Jesus was helping Peter move on from his failure. Peter had denied Jesus three times – and now he had the opportunity to undo it – three times. 'Yes, Lord I love you – you know that I do,' Peter replied, each time stronger than the last.

All Jesus was interested in was seeing Peter back on the road again. It's the same for us. He did it for Peter and he always wants to do it for us. But how?

If we confess our sins

We know God never winks at sin. It is too much of a stench in his nostrils for that to happen. And its impact is too profound to be ignored. This is why the death of Jesus was so essential. It was a sacrifice for all sin for all time even for my sins that are still to come.

The death of Jesus provides a limitless reserve of forgiveness for the future – against which we can cash each and every IOU that our continuing sinful behaviour creates. Obviously this only applies to you if you have taken that step of saving faith. It is only then that you have an endless line of credit on your account waiting to be drawn down.

How does that work? Another one of Jesus' great friends, John wrote, 'If we confess our sins, he is faithful and just and will forgive us our sins and purify us from all unrighteousness'.[5]

We don't become perfect, even with Jesus at the centre of our lives. That is the purpose of confession – to clear out those bits of grit that would build up and hinder our day-to-day relationship with God. Jesus hinted at this when he talked of starting the day with a bath that washed us from head to toe – but with us still needing to wash the daily dust and grime from our feet.[6]

Of course, 'confessing our sins' means a lot more than mechanically running through a list. It is about 'doing a Peter'.

Peter was truly sorry for what he had done. And the sorrow he felt was linked to the love he had for Jesus and the hurt he had caused him.

Confession for us comes out of that same kind of deep, personal sorrow for the damage done to our relationship with God. And a genuine longing not to repeat the past. It involves agreeing with God that what we did, said or thought was wrong. And thanking him for forgiving us.

When we do genuinely confess our sins to God – as Peter did – he acts faithfully and justly. This is possible because the payment for our wrongdoing has been made. We are again made clean – as clean as Jesus.

Can we do what we like and then say sorry?

Some people are daft enough to suggest that, because 'sorry' is enough, we can get away with murder in God's eyes. But how could anyone who has received such love at so great a cost then wilfully exploit it?

If someone risked life and limb to save me from some terrible fate, would I steal their wallet? If someone offered a blank cheque to pay off all my bills – at great personal expense – would I first go on a lavishly indulgent spending spree?

In the same way, if I have really understood the passion of God towards me how could I possibly keep hammering the nails into the hands and feet of Jesus knowingly and willingly? No way.

Some of the first followers of Jesus so misunderstood how

much God loved to forgive that they decided to do him a favour – by giving him lots of opportunities to do so. They deliberately did wrong so God would have the pleasure of showering them with forgiveness.

However bizarre that may sound, at least they had grasped the big issue – that God delights in forgiving. Like the story Jesus told about the father who welcomed back his waster of a son, God will do the same for us, time and time again. But like that son, we would never exploit the love of the Father.

One step backwards – two steps forward

Think for a moment of your new life with God as though it were a garden. Over the past few pages of this book we have discovered how sweet the flower of God's mercy smells. And how God helps us deal with the weeds that grow in our life.

But there's even more to it than that. God's plan is not just for you to exist but to flourish and grow. How? Please follow me to the greenhouse.

Chapter 16

IT'S A PLOT

How will your garden grow?

We begin our journey of faith by getting to know God – and continue by getting to know him better. But how do we do it? Let me run a couple of questions past you – in the hope that they will expand your horizons and expectations.

If God intends us to have a relationship with him, how can we get to know him better?

If God is a person he must have plans, purposes and intentions – for us and for others. How can we get in on them?

Let's go digging up the dirt for some answers.

Nurturing our relationship with God

As we are thinking of you as a newish follower of Jesus it could be appropriate to use the imagery of the nursery to make things clear. But I find all this talk about projectile vomiting, potty training and grazed knees somewhat off-putting. Instead, let's transplant you into a garden.

Please forgive me if I flog the horticultural image to death over the following pages. But there's so much we can understand about our relationship with God and his people through the insights of a garden.

We've already seen that our life with God is to be a relationship. So how do we make that work?

It's good to talk

Not that long ago Prince Charles hit the headlines for allegedly talking to plants. True or not, there are those who do – defending themselves with the claim that plants have feelings too. These person-to-plant chit chats are supposed to make both parties healthier.

That all sounds completely herbiscus to me. But whether or not a plant benefits from a friendly chat, our relationship with God does. Such conversation is like the oxygen that every healthy plant needs to grow.

Most people call this prayer – but the word can conjure up some strange images. We may assume prayer involves learning a whole new vocabulary, going to special places, reciting things written long ago, doing something with our body we are not particularly used to and even putting on a special voice.

None of that need be true. Think of it this way.

Prayer is not a ritual. There are those who can only ever enter Queen Elizabeth's presence fully booted and suited and accompanied by a full monty of pomp and circumstance. Yet, down through the years, some have swooped unannounced into her presence, wearing Harrods jim-jams, and yelling 'Mummy'.

In the same way, while God is the creator and sustainer of all things, he has also made himself known as our Father in heaven. And that's the basis of our time in his presence. It's not an audience with a head of state, but time with a loving father.

Of course, our visiting rights with God need to be respectful, but we do go to him as his child and that's how he wants it.

When chatting with friends there are times when we are serious – even crying. Times when we are earnest. And times just to enjoy each other's company. Our conversations with God can be much the same.

Prayer is a conversation. Our talk time with God is not meant to be like him listening to the radio – all one way. God wants to share his thoughts and feelings back to us too.

Sure, God is ever ready to listen to the words on our lips and the unspoken feelings of our heart. But he'd also like us to give him the space to prompt our spirit and touch our mind.

A friend of mine clearly remembers driving down the road chatting with God and telling him how much he loved him. Suddenly – like a starburst – God showed him how much he loved him too. My friend thought his heart would explode.

We can share even our deepest feelings with God – after all, he knows them anyway. And you're never going to catch him by surprise. He won't respond 'I never knew that!'

Getting kick-started. Perhaps you are thinking, 'But where do I start?' Forgive me, but I am going to have to go to the nursery for a moment. The simple answer is, start with a few coos and dribbles.

What makes you so sure God's fussed about hearing a long eloquent speech from you anyway? Have you ever been present when some infant burbled its first Dadda? Remember the shrieks of joy and ecstasy that broke out? Take it from me, God will be equally happy over your first infant mumblings.

Food for thought

Back to plants and another thing they need – food. Whether you think in terms of rain or Baby Bio the principle is the same – strong plants get that way through nourishment.

Of course, prayer is part of that process. But the mainstay is God's written word – the Bible. You want to know God better, to see how he acts, to know what excites him, makes him mad and what he does about it? Well, God's put it all in writing for you.

The Bible is not just some tired old historical tome written centuries ago by irrelevant people. The Bible is actually 'alive'. In fact, the Bible describes itself as '. . . living and active. Sharper than any double-edged sword, it penetrates even to dividing soul and spirit, joints and marrow; it judges the thoughts and attitudes of the heart.'[1] And you thought it was just a book?

The Bible is God's message to you and the world. Through it he wants to draw us closer to himself and give us a new quality of life. And it's one of the main ways we discover the details of his character, plans and purposes for us and others.

No wonder the Bible continues to outsell every other book worldwide every week. How can you make the most of it?

Read chunks at a time. The Bible was written to be consumed banquet-style, not snacked on like calorie-counting nibbles. So try to read it that way. Take whole sections and read them at one go.

In this way it's like drinking a whole barrel of wholesome fertiliser – it fills you, feeds you, and helps you keep on growing.

Start with something like the stories of Jesus' life, which are found in the first four books of the New Testament. And get your hands on a modern translation that's easy to read.

Read with a willingness to discover and act. Ask yourself, why was this written down? What did it have to say to those who first read it? And how does it apply to you, your family, work and friends?

Expect God to nudge you as you read. Notice where it makes you go 'wow'. And where 'ouch'. And figure out what you should do about it.

At times the Bible will be food for your soul. At others it will be the gardener's pruning shears. Both are essential for healthy growth.

Memorise some of it. When you come to a bit that particularly strikes you, find a way to lock it into your memory. Jot it down and stick it by your mirror, turn it into a PC screen saver, programme it into your mobile phone display. Anything that will help you let it fill your mind and help you to chew on it.

One reason for doing this may be to reinforce something God wants you to be sure you have grasped and made your own. Let's say you have a certain fear – like that of facing a new challenge at work – you might want to memorise something that expresses the way God will always be there for you.

Read it with others. Don't get too 'driven' about spending hours reading the Bible by yourself – particularly if reading is not something you do anyway. It's only been for the past two hundred years or so that the followers of Jesus have been able to do this anyway.

What will make a difference is to dig into the Bible with two or three other people. Take it in turns to look for 'ahs' and 'ouches'. Share what you discover together. And do it often.

Be ready to pollinate

The reason there are so many flowers is all down to pollination. The breeze blows, pollen spreads and new life begins.

The good news about Jesus – which you have experienced for yourself – spreads in the same kind of way. The breeze of

God's Spirit blows, what we know about Jesus makes a journey to someone else and, sometimes, it takes root and grows.

You are part of that process. It's nothing to lose sleep over or break into a sweat about. It's part of normal life.

But remember two things.

Don't get up people's noses. You know what happens when pollen gets up nostrils. So don't do it. Be a fragrance, not an irritant.

You don't have to dump pollen all over people who don't want it. But you'll notice that the more attractive the flower of your life grows, the more people will want to have a sniff.

Choose your moment. There is a season when pollen is most likely to 'take'. It's the season when the other plant is ready for it. In the same way, there will be the times when people want to hear. And these are the best moments to explain what has become real to you.

Remember, just like pollination in nature, God is part of the process. He's the one who prepares people for what they hear and helps you say what needs to be said. Part of the good news to us is the final promise Jesus made to the disciples – his pollinators. He promised, 'I will be with you always, even until the end of the world'.[2] And that includes you.

Join a fragrant bunch

Plants don't exist by themselves. They are part of an intricate ecological system. The same is true of those who follow Jesus. Our faith may be personal but it's not solitary.

Being part of a group who are travelling in the same direction as you is not an option. It's an absolute essential.

We need others for our spiritual survival and have a part to play in theirs.

There's strength in numbers. Take a stick and bend it and it will quickly snap in half. Take ten or twenty, place them together like one thick branch, and it would take a chainsaw to do the same job.

The same is true for us. Try to make a go of our relationship with Jesus on our own and we are vulnerable to the pressure that can snap our faith in two. But there is strength in numbers. So use it.

We need others to encourage us down the path of life and to help hold us up when things get tough, confusing and even discouraging. Just like Dorothy had Toto, the Scarecrow, Tin-man, and the Lion – so we too have one another to journey with down life's yellow brick and mud-spattered road. We dance and sing, 'We're off to see the Maker – the wonderful Maker of all . . .'

And we will get there one day – but we will only do it together.

The big picture

What I've spoken about so far is the importance of you being part of a small group of like-minded people – like Dorothy and chums. But the picture is far bigger than that. As a follower of Jesus you are into something vast. Let me try to give you the panoramic perspective.

Are you familiar with the children's television phenomenon called Power Rangers? In this Japanese-style kick-fest, five Californian kids use their karate-chop powers to protect the planet. Much fun is had by the fabulous five while they prance and pummel themselves in true Bruce Lee fashion – while wearing coloured leotards no respectable planet-saver would be seen dead in.

The thing is, when fighting individually, it becomes quickly apparent they couldn't beat their way out of a children's birthday party. They get pulverised by the nifty nasties invading their world.

But watch out. Because when these kids get in trouble they fit together to make one huge great mechanical monster so scary that even the great Godzilla would soil himself at the sight of it.

These five punchers are useless on their own – but by becoming united there is no stopping them. And this is what has happened to those of us who are followers of Jesus. We have become one. We are called the Church – which isn't a building or a programme of activities but a united body primed for action.

Like the Power Rangers, by ourselves we are beaten, but together we can be all that God intends. Even without the coloured leotards.

One of the first Christian leaders, the Apostle Paul, used an image a little closer to home than these Jurassic juveniles. He called the church 'the body of Christ'. He wanted us to see ourselves as the limbs or organs of one body – each with a different role to play but essential to the others.

The global garden

This body is far bigger than you can ever imagine. To think in gardening terms again, it is a vast plantation stretching from horizon to horizon and beyond. And that is only a part of it.

The garden of history. The Church is the only organisation that never loses a member through death. But don't think in terms of the believers of old now being some decaying compost heap in the sky. They are celebrating with the whole population of heaven and are just as alive as we are. In fact, even more so.

They include young and old, rich and poor, unknown and mega-famous. Heaven is full of history makers, life changers, unknown and seemingly insignificant people too and those whose shadow we are not worthy to shelter under. They are all our people. Trillions of them. We are part of that magnificent Body and they are part of us.

The garden of geography. Worldwide there is a vast multitude of different expressions of the Body of Jesus.

In China they meet secretly in homes due to persecution. In Latin America it takes stadium-sized buildings to cater for congregations – with as many as 80,000 meeting to worship and learn together.

Elsewhere the Body meet in hotels, public halls, schools, church buildings, the open air, gymnasiums, cathedrals and under bamboo roofs.

Some worship in silence, others to a Latin beat or with the fervour of rock 'n roll – and seemingly everything and anything in between. Some use written prayers, some seem to busk it, while others use a laptop and LCD projector.

Every major culture is represented in the worldwide church. The Body of Jesus is as varied as the flora in London's Kew Gardens.

This vast company of people all have one thing in common – they worship Jesus as Lord of their lives and have come to know God as a personal friend and Father. Day by day, week by week, they celebrate their new life with Jesus. And you're a part of it.

The reason for the garden

Gardens and bodies exist for a purpose. They are not there just to 'be' but also to 'do'. So far as the Body of Jesus is concerned we exist to do what he did. Literally to be his body

– together bringing and being good news wherever we are and whenever we can.

There have been times when the church has failed miserably in that role. But there have also been times when the compassion of Jesus through his Body on earth has transformed relationships, families, communities and even nations.

Hospitals, hospices, the end of the slave trade, major social reforms protecting children, women and the disadvantaged – and much more – all have their roots in the Body of Jesus at work.

We are to be salt

Jesus said his followers were to have the same impact as salt.[3] When scattered in society we are to act like a preservative – holding back the growth of evil and decay, acting like a purifying agent to make things cleaner.

As salt we are to bring healing to wounded and hurting people. And sometimes, like salt, we may even sting a little as we stand against evil and injustice.

We are to be a light set on a hill

The impact of what we do as the body of Jesus is meant to be seen. Jesus said we were to be like a bright light – showing the way.[4]

This does not involve making a claim to be superior or more important than anyone else. It just means we are to be a living example of the way life is intended to be – and so help others find the way for themselves.

What's it all for anyway?

Ultimately what should motivate us to live as God intends? In the end there is only one thing – our love for Jesus because of who he is and all he has done for us. Let me illustrate what that can mean.

The Bible paints a graphic picture of Jesus as a bridegroom – with the Church, us, as his bride.[5] One day, as the end captions of history roll, we will see him face to face for all eternity at our great wedding feast.

To capture what that means you need to understand the wedding customs of Jesus' time. When a girl became promised in marriage she was given the cloth to make her own wedding garment. And she went diligently and lovingly to work.

Hour upon hour she would labour. Every stitch, tuck and piece of intricate embroidery demonstrated the love she had for her future husband. There was no other motivation. That's why she did it all. Love for him.

Not long ago I saw something very much like this at first hand. From the vantage point of being the groom's father I watched my son's bride arrive alongside him. She had devoted hours of detailed planning and preparation into this one moment – just to demonstrate her love. And the message was written all over her radiant face – 'I did this all for you because I love you.'

It's the same with all we do as the bride of Jesus. It's not just that we want to live cleaner, better lives. Or to make our street, neighbourhood, workplace, and world a better place to be. Or that we need to make ourselves useful until the time comes. It's because each act – wherever we are and whatever we are doing – can contribute to our wedding garment, which displays our love for Jesus.

One day we will meet Jesus face to face. His body will carry the marks of his love. And we will be wearing the evidence of ours. There can be no better reason for serving him than that he is worth it. And he is.

His love is truly beyond belief.

Notes

Finding Your Way Through the References

This book claims Jesus said and did certain things. You need to know we're not making it up – and to read it for yourself if you wish. So we've shown you where to look in the record of his life that's included in the Bible.

For example, to find Luke 3:22, use the table of contents in the front of a Bible to find the 'book' of Luke. The number '3' shows the chapter of Luke, while '22' refers to the verse within that chapter. Where we quote directly, we use either the New International Version or the Contemporary English Version (CEV) – easy-to-read translations.

Chapter 1

1. Stewart Steven, *The Mail on Sunday*, 27 December 1998

Chapter 4

1. John 14:9
2. John 10:30

3. Matthew 10:40
4. John 8:58
5. Luke 5:17–26
6. Mark 14:61–62

Chapter 6

1. John 19:32
2. John 19:38–40
3. John 20:15–16
4. John 20:3–8
5. John 20:19
6. Luke 4:13–33
7. John 20:25–29

Chapter 7

1. Genesis 4:7
2. Isaiah 53:6
3. Isaiah 59:2

Chapter 8

1. Luke 23:4
2. Mark 10:33–34
3. John 12:32
4. Matthew 20:28
5. John 10:18
6. Matthew 26:53
7. Matthew 27:30
8. Matthew 27:12–14
9. Matthew 27:50
10. Micah 5:2
11. Isaiah 7:14

12. Psalm 41:9
13. Zechariah 11:12
14. Isaiah 50:6
15. Psalm 22:16
16. Zechariah 12:10
17. Psalm 22:18
18. Psalm 34:20
19. Isaiah 53:9
20. Psalm 16:10
21. John 1:29
22. John 19:30
23. Amos 8:9
24. Luke 23:44–45
25. Isaiah 53:5
26. Matthew 27:46

Chapter 9

1. John 14:6

Chapter 10

1. Quoted in *It Makes Sense*, Stephen Gaukroger, Scripture Union

Chapter 11

1. *Sunday Telegraph*, 25 May 1997
2. Luke 23:43 (CEV)
3. John 14:2
4. John 14:3 (CEV)
5. Matthew 6:19
6. Luke 10:20
7. Matthew 25:32

8. Matthew 3:12
9. Matthew 7:13
10. John 6:40

Chapter 12

1. John 3:36
2. Luke 15:11–32

Chapter 13

1. Luke 14:25–35
2. Luke 22:20
3. Luke 14:27
4. Luke 14:33
5. Luke 14:26
6. John 14:15 (CEV)

Chapter 14

1. Romans 8:11
2. 2 Corinthians 1:22
3. Ephesians 3:16
4. John 3:1–21
5. John 17:1
6. Luke 3:22
7. Matthew 12:31
8. Matthew 6:9
9. Mark 14:36
10. John 10:16–18

Chapter 15

1. John 10:10 (CEV)
2. Luke 10:27
3. John 1:12
4. John 21:1–17
5. 1 John 1:9
6. John 13:1–10

Chapter 16

1. Hebrews 4:12
2. Matthew 28:20
3. Matthew 5:13
4. Matthew 5:14
5. Revelation 19:6–9